Edexcel GCSE

History A: The Making of the Modern World

Unit 3B: War and the transformation of British society c.1931–51

endorsed for
edexcel

Author:
Jane Shuter

Series Editors:
Nigel Kelly
Angela Leonard

Updated for the
2013 specifications by:
Jane Shuter

ALWAYS LEARNING

PEARSON

Contents: delivering the Edexcel GCSE History A (The Making of the Modern World) specification Unit 3B

Key terms are emboldened in the text, and can be found in the glossary.

Welcome to the course

Welcome to Modern World History! Studying this subject will help you to understand the world you live in: the events of the last century can help to explain the problems and opportunities that exist in the world today.

How to use this book

There are four units in the course and each is worth 25% of the whole GCSE. This book covers Unit 3B: War and the transformation of British society c.1931–51. There are four key topics in this unit and you will study *all four*.

- **Key Topic 1:** The impact of the Depression 1931–39
- **Key Topic 2:** Britain at war 1939–45
- **Key Topic 3:** The Home Front 1939–45
- **Key Topic 4:** Labour in power 1945–51

Zone in: how to get into the perfect 'zone' for revision.

Planning zone: tips and advice on how to plan revision effectively.

Know zone: the facts you need to know, memory tips and exam-style practice for every section.

Don't panic zone: last-minute revision tips.

Exam zone: what to expect on the exam paper.

Zone out: what happens after the exams.

Top Tips provide handy hints on how to apply what you have learned and how to remember key information and concepts.

Top tip

When asked what they can learn from a source, students who do well will make an *inference* – they will work out the implications of what the source is saying and refer to the source to support it. So, for Source A one inference would be that they had good warning of the enemy coming: they were in the air and looking for them.

Watch out!

The various ways of referring to Russia under communist rule can be confusing. It is sometimes called the USSR (Union of Socialist Soviet Republics) and sometimes the Soviet Union. Other people refer to it as Russia.

Watch out! These warn you about common mistakes and misconceptions that students often make.

Build better answers The Know Zone Build better answers pages at the end of each section include an exam-style question with a student answer, comments and an improved answer so that you can see how to improve your own writing.

Build better answers give you an opportunity to answer exam-style questions. They include tips for what a basic ■, good ⬤ and excellent △ answer will contain.

Build better answers

Exam question: What can you learn from Source D about the effects of *Blitzkrieg*? (6 marks)

When you are asked what you can learn from a source or sources, you are expected to make *inferences*. This means you work something out from the information in the source; you don't just copy it.

■ **A basic answer (level 1)** just repeats information from the source (for example, *it tells me that there was bombing, waves of planes and the soldiers lining up fighting the German army*).

⬤ **A good answer (level 2)** m

Build better answers

Question 1
Tip: Question 1 will ask you what you can learn about a particular topic from the sources provided. Be careful not just to copy information from the source. You need to make inferences from the sources – work something out based on the information in them. Let's look at an example (Source C on page 21).

'What can you learn from Source C about the impact of the Jarrow Crusade?' (6 marks)

Student answer	Comments
The source tells me that the MP making the speech saw the march as a boy and remembers it.	This answer mainly reproduces information from the source and would get very few marks.

Let's rewrite the answer, making inferences and showing how the source helped us make them.

| The source tells me that the MP making the speech saw the march as a boy and remembers it. S_ _must have made an impression on him._ _it suggests the Jarrow Crusade had_ | In this answer there are two inferences made from the source (shown underlined) using detail from the source |

Unit 3: The source enquiry: an introduction

What is Unit 3 about?

The Unit 3 topics are very different from those in Units 1 and 2. To start with, you are never going to be asked just to recall historical information you have learned. If you find yourself sitting in an examination telling the story of what happened in a particular historical event, you are almost certainly not doing the right thing! Unlike Units 1 and 2, Unit 3 is not about recalling or describing key features. Nor is it about using your knowledge to construct an argument about why things happened – or what the consequences of an action were. Instead, Unit 3 topics are about understanding the importance of sources in the study of history.

History as a subject is not just about learning a series of facts and repeating them in an examination. It is actually a process of enquiry. Historians understand that our historical knowledge comes from evidence from the past ('sources'). Historians have to piece together what has happened in the past from these sources. They need to interpret the sources to build up the historical picture. That is what you will be looking at in Unit 3.

Sources can sometimes be interpreted in a number of ways. They will also have been created for a variety of purposes. This means that historians also have to make judgements about the reliability of sources. You will learn ways of judging whether the information in a source is accurate or not. To make judgements about sources, you need to have some knowledge about the topic the sources relate to. You will need to use this information and the information in the sources to answer many of the questions in the examination. Don't tell the whole story, but select information from your own knowledge to support what you are saying about the source.

The examination

In the examination you will be given a collection of sources to study. Then you will be asked five questions. These five questions will test your understanding of interpreting sources. The good news is that each year the individual questions will always test the same skill. So Question 1 will always be about making an inference. The table at the top of the next page shows how this works.

Question	Marks	Type of question
1	6	Making inferences from sources
2	8	Considering the purpose of a source
3	10	Explaining causation using a source and own knowledge
4	10	Evaluating the reliability of sources
5	16	Evaluating a hypothesis
	+3	An additional 3 marks for spelling, punctuation and grammar are available in Question 5.

So before you study the historical topic from which your sources will be drawn, let's make sure you know how to answer each question type.

Making inferences from sources

When you read or look at a source and you understand its content, you are 'comprehending' that source. When you make a judgement from what the source says or shows, you are 'making an inference'. Let us look at a source to see what that means.

Source A — *From a book about the Jarrow Crusade, written by a historian in 2005.*

> The Jarrow Crusade was one of four hunger marches to London in 1936. They were: the National Hunger March, the Jarrow Crusade, the National League of the Blind march and the Scottish veterans' march. They passed through the same towns and sometimes crossed paths. They were ignored in the same way by the government and were all carefully watched by the police.

In the examination, the sort of question you might be asked would be:

'What can you learn from Source A about unemployment in 1936?'

You could say: '*People went on hunger marches.*' That is true, but it doesn't take much working out, does it? It isn't an inference either, because that is exactly what the source says.

An example of an inference about unemployment would be: '*Unemployment must have been a serious problem because the source says there were four different hunger marches. That suggests people had no money for food because they were not working – and the number of marches suggests a lot of unemployment.*' Can you see the difference?

Considering the purpose of a source

It is important for historians to understand why sources have been created. Sometimes people are just recording what has happened (as in a diary), but sometimes they are created to get a message across. For example, when an artist paints a picture, he or she may be doing so in order to get a message across. Let's look at an example.

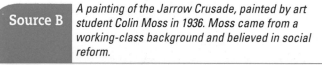

Source B — A painting of the Jarrow Crusade, painted by art student Colin Moss in 1936. Moss came from a working-class background and believed in social reform.

In the examination, the sort of question you might be asked about this painting is:

'*Why do you think the artist painted this picture?*'

You could say: '*to show the Jarrow March*', but that is a very weak answer. A good answer would involve looking at the detail in the poster and working out why the artist painted this march – or a hunger march at all. You need to consider the artist's purpose. You could start with the message he's sending. The men are marching away from the picture. You don't see their faces, but they are marching and look determined and organised. The policeman isn't having to do anything to control them.

So by the way the artist shows them (including the rain; it didn't rain every day) the artist wants you to feel sympathy for the marchers, to feel supportive.

The caption tells you he's a working-class student who supported social reform, so this confirms the purpose is to encourage sympathy for the marchers.

Source C — *A government statement made during the marches.*

Ministers have considered the fact that there are a number of 'marches' on London in progress or being planned. In the opinion of the government these marches can do no good for the causes they say they represent and are likely to cause unnecessary hardship for those taking part in them. Processions to London cannot have any right in our democracy to influence government policy.

Explaining causation

Question 3 asks you to explain causation using a source and your own knowledge. Read Source C.

In the examination, the sort of question you might be asked is:

'*Use Source C and your own knowledge to explain why the government opposed the Jarrow marchers.*'

Your task is to use the source and your own knowledge to explain why the government opposed the Jarrow marchers. You must explain how the source shows this **and** add more from your own knowledge.

From the source you could extract the following reasons: they can't do any good; they'll make things worse for the marchers; marchers should not influence government policy. **Explain** how what is said shows government opposition: they are opposed to actions aimed at forcing the government to act.

Now you need to add something from your own knowledge. You could explain why they say it will make things worse for the marchers (they wouldn't get unemployment benefit) and add that the government was worried about political unrest from this and earlier marches.

I don't think the decision of the council not to welcome the marchers represents the feeling of the people of Northallerton. This march is the finest organised I have ever seen. It is our duty to spare no effort to help our unfortunate comrades and I think the churches of this country should have led the march and taken it right to London as an appeal not only to the Government but also to the common humanity in man.

Evaluating the reliability of sources

Question 4 asks you to consider how reliable two sources are as evidence of something. You must refer to both sources and use your own knowledge. Let's look at Source C and Source D (treat each source in the same way in the exam). In the examination, the sort of question you might be asked is:

'How reliable are Sources C and D as evidence about support for the Jarrow March?'

You could say: 'Source D was written by a vicar who supported the march,' OR 'Source C came from the government who were against the march.' But these are just general statements. To do well you need to ask who has produced the source and why. You also need to consider how representative of support (or the lack of it) the sources are likely to be. For example, *the caption to Source D implies that Northallerton town council were against the march, even if the speaker was in favour of it. You could also point out the speaker's job: he's a churchman, but that doesn't mean all churchmen supported the march – he says as much in the speech.* On the other hand, the fact Source C refers to 'a number of marches', suggesting that the idea of marching to protest had support.

Evaluating a hypothesis

Question 5 asks how far you agree with a view put forward by one of the sources in the exam paper. You will be expected to use several sources and your own knowledge to decide this. This is the sort of question you might be asked:

Source E suggests the Jarrow Crusade had a big impact. How far do you agree with this interpretation? Use your own knowledge, Sources A, D and E and any other sources you find helpful to explain your answer.

The best answers make a judgement about how far they agree with the interpretation. They then provide detail from the sources **and** their own knowledge to support this judgement. For example: *'Source A tells us there were several marches, lists them and suggests that they were covering similar routes with similar aims. It seems to imply that the Jarrow march was just one of several, nothing special. But the Jarrow march must have been special to many people. Source E shows it being referred to in 1951 – not all the marches, just the Jarrow one. Source D suggests their level of organisation had an impact – people wanted to help them. But that would be a short-term impact: help on the march. Did it get them jobs? We know a few people got jobs outside Jarrow and a small steelworks (only employing 200 people) was set up. Neither of these things would have happened without the march. However, the government, in Source C, seem pretty clear that they think the marches should not influence what they do and they did nothing to provide jobs. So the impact was more emotional than productive.'*

Key Topic 1: The impact of the Depression

In 1929, the US stock market collapsed. The USA had been supporting the European economy since the First World War ended in 1918. Now, the USA had to trade less, stop lending and call for the repayment of its loans to other countries. Britain was among these countries. The Depression in the USA had a terrible effect on some parts of Britain's economy. Industries sold less, therefore made less money, so had to sack workers or pay them considerably less and restrict their working hours. This produced a downward economic spiral where these problems fed each other over and over again. One of the most obvious signs of this was the rise in unemployment.

In this Key Topic, you will study:

- the growth of unemployment and the government response
- the experience of the unemployed
- case study: the Jarrow Crusade.

You will see how unemployment was different in different industries and parts of Britain. You will also see how the unemployed campaigned for work (stressing that it was work they wanted, not more benefits). You will consider the action the government took to help the unemployed – and the effects of their actions.

Your case study of the Jarrow Crusade will examine the Crusade itself as well as opposition and public reaction to it. It will also consider why the Crusade was so important.

Britain in the 1920s: background to the Depression

At the end of the First World War, the only financial help for the unemployed was National Insurance Benefit, set up in 1911 to cover workers in a few industries, such as shipbuilding, where work was not steady. Workers and their employers paid into an Unemployment Fund. If work dried up, the fund paid benefit for up to 15 weeks. In November 1918, the government set up an Out-of-Work Donation Scheme (often called 'the dole'), which paid a small amount of benefit. The scheme was set up to help returning soldiers and war workers who could not find employment. During the 1920s, the economy was struggling and unemployment was a problem. Although women had worked during the war, they were expected to give up their jobs to the returning men. Most workers, and therefore most of the unemployed, were men – often men with families to support.

The **Depression** made unemployment in Britain worse. In 1929, there were 1.5 million unemployed. In 1930, it had risen to 2.4 million. Some newer industries, such as car and electrical goods manufacturing, did hire more workers – but these were mainly based were mainly based in the south and west of the country. Workers in badly affected industries and the unemployed protested in various ways. They collected petitions and wrote individually to the government, asking for work. They wrote to the newspapers, highlighting the problems. They also regularly marched to London to protest to the government about conditions. These '**hunger marches**' were almost all organised by the National Unemployed Workers' Movement (NUWM), set up in 1921. They tried hard to make the point that the unemployed were not lazy, but wanted work more than **benefits**. Meanwhile, the state, and the Unemployment Fund, were paying out more and more money in various benefits, as work was not to be found.

Source A Welsh miners photographed in November 1927, on their arrival in London to protest about the government (led by Stanley Baldwin) extending miners' legal working from 7 to 8 hours a day. Think about why the man to the right of the banner is wearing his medals.

Exam-style question

What was the purpose of Source A? Use details of the photograph and your own knowledge to explain your answer. **(8 marks)**

Source B A song sung by striking clothing workers, mostly women, in London in 1928. To 'stick' was to stay out on strike, not return to work.

We've never had decent wages
And always done our work well
How long must this go on?
More work – less pay
But every dog will have its day
We'll stick, by gum, by golly
The bosses they'll be sorry.

Unemployment in Britain in the 1930s

Learning objectives

In this chapter you will learn about:
- levels and distribution of unemployment in Britain in the 1930s
- making inferences from sources.

Unemployment in the 1930s was highest in the coal, iron and steel, cotton and shipbuilding industries, in the north and east of England and in Scotland and Wales. By 1932, 34.5% of all miners and 62% of all shipbuilders were unemployed. Unemployment was not spread evenly. When pits and shipyards closed, the villages that served them became almost entirely unemployed.

Meanwhile, 80% of all new factories built from 1932 to 1937 were in London or nearby. They were usually for new industries, such as car making. These factories ran mostly on electricity, not coal, so did not help the coal industry by increasing demand for fuel. But they did keep employment up in London and the south east. The chemical industry, for example, had 17.6% unemployment in 1932, which was low compared to mining or shipbuilding.

If you lived in the right part of the country and worked in the right industry, the Depression could almost pass you by. There were people who were living well and felt untouched by the Depression, even if they did feel sorry for those who were hit hard by it.

Source A	Unemployment in Britain, 1920–38.

Date	Unemployed, on National Insurance	Total unemployed	Total unemployed as % of all those able to work
1929	1,250,000	1,503,000	8%
1930	1,979,000	2,379,000	12.3%
1931	2,705,000	3,252,000	16.4%
1932	2,828,000	3,400,000	17%
1933	2,567,000	3,087,000	15.4%
1934	2,170,000	2,609,000	12.9%
1935	2,027,000	2,437,000	12%
1936	1,749,000	2,100,000	10.2%
1937	1,482,000	1,776,000	8.5%
1938	1,800,000	2,164,000	10.1%

Source: W. R. Garside, British Unemployment 1919–1939 (1990), Table 2, p.5 (adapted), © Cambridge University Press 1990, reproduced with permission.

Source B	From a 1973 interview with Richard Etheridge, who became a union leader in the Austin car factory in Birmingham in the 1940s.

I grew up in Birmingham during the Depression. Out of a class of 30 of us boys, we were lucky if one got a job when they left. I worked for a while in a laboratory, making up formulas for various industries. I got very sick of that. Then our family started up an all-night café and I left to work there. I started to meet people involved in the **trade union** movement and got interested in that.

| Source C | The percentage of people paying National Insurance in each region who were able to work but were unemployed, 1929–38. | | | | | | | |

Date	London	South east	South west	Midlands	North east	North west	Scotland	Wales
1929	5.6	5.6	8.1	9.3	13.7	13.3	12.1	19.3
1930	8.1	8	10.4	14.7	20.2	23.8	18.5	25.9
1931	12.2	12	14.5	20.3	27.4	28.2	26.6	32.4
1932	13.5	14.3	17.1	20.1	28.5	25.8	27.7	36.5
1933	11.8	11.5	15.7	17.4	26	23.5	26.1	34.6
1934	9.2	8.7	13.1	12.9	22.1	20.8	23.1	32.3
1935	8.5	8.1	11.6	11.2	20.7	19.7	21.3	31.2
1936	7.2	7.3	9.4	9.2	16.8	17.1	18.7	29.4
1937	6.4	6.7	7.8	7.3	11.1	14	16	23.3
1938	8	8	8.2	10.3	13.6	17.9	16.4	24.8

| Source D | A hunger march in London in 1930. This march was organised by the National Unemployed Workers' Movement (NUWM). What do you think the slogan means? |

Activities

1 a What can you learn from Source A about unemployment in Britain in the 1930s?

   b Use Source C to make a graph of unemployment in Britain in the 1930s.

   c Write a sentence explaining the patterns the graph shows.

2 Write a piece of advice to someone time-travelling back to live in the 1930s for a few years. Tell them which part of the country to live in and why.

3 Research the factors that led to the high unemployment of the 1930s. Use these prompts to help you:

   a Structural weakness of key industries

   b Keeping pace with new technologies

   c Old and new industries.

Government reactions

Learning objectives

In this chapter you will learn about:
- how the government tried to deal with the problems of unemployment
- considering the purpose of a source.

Labour in power

In 1929, Labour came to power, with Ramsay MacDonald as prime minister. The government needed money. It was in debt and the Depression made it hard to borrow money to cover spending. So the government made huge spending cuts (for example it cut government workers' wages by 10–15 %) but still could not pay the 1929 unemployment benefits without borrowing. Worse still, the Unemployment Insurance Act would push up the cost of benefit payments. Under this act, more people were entitled to benefit and claimants no longer had to prove they had been 'actively seeking work'. This clause had been used to exclude many people from benefit. The act was fairer, and necessary, but expensive. So, in August 1931, government **ministers** discussed cutting benefit rates by 15% and setting up a '**means test**'. This test let officials visit a benefit claimant's home to examine the living conditions (to make sure he was poor enough) and to know the savings and earning of all family members, not just the person claiming benefit. Most ministers refused to accept the proposals. They said the cuts would cause too much hardship and the 'means test' was too humiliating. The government collapsed.

The National Government

MacDonald, as prime minister, set up a National Government of moderate Labour, Liberal and Conservative MPs. This National Government held a general election in October – and won. So what would it do for the unemployed?

The 1934 Unemployment Act

By the end of 1931, the government had cut the unemployment benefit rate by 10% and set up the means test. In 1934 the Unemployment Act clarified the differences between types of benefit.

- National Insurance (NI) benefit was the right of everyone paying their NI contributions. There was no means test. However, this benefit was only paid for 15 weeks.
- The 'dole' was a lower payment given to unemployed people who had not paid NI contributions OR who had had 15 weeks of NI benefit. A National Unemployment Assistance Board ran the dole from taxes. Claimants still had to pass the means test.

Special Areas

The government knew some parts of the country had been hit harder than others. In 1934 it passed the Special Areas Act, giving £2 million to help in these areas: Scotland, Tyneside (in the north-east), Cumberland (in the north-west) and South Wales. Local authorities applied for money to be spent on 'economic development' and 'social improvement'. This money was not much to solve the problems in these areas and some local authorities made more applications and spent more wisely than others. The government knew the money wasn't enough and in 1936 debated ways to give more help, but the help wasn't always well-thought-out. It allowed industries to apply directly for money but in worst-hit areas the industry had already collapsed and so could not apply.

The 1937 Special Areas (Amendment) Act gave tax cuts and low rents to businesses that moved into Special Areas. But these were seldom enough to tempt businesses to relocate.

Source A	Part of a speech by Labour MP George Lansbury, in a debate in parliament, 4 November 1932. Do you think Lansbury was in the National Government?

The cost of unemployment, the £600 million or so, is a fraction of the real cost of unemployment to this nation. There is the cost to families and to individuals; all their savings poured out and gone. You cannot starve people (although it is semi-starvation for many now). I appeal to the Government. We think the amounts are too low, and should be increased. It is said we cannot afford it. We cannot afford the physical, mental and moral deterioration to people who cannot live on what is provided.

A poster for the National Government for the 1935 election.

Activities

1 Make a table with the headings below and complete it for major changes and laws affecting the unemployed in the 1930s.

Date	Measure	What it did
1930	Unemployment Insurance Act	gave more people benefit no longer had to prove 'actively seeking work'

---

examzone

Build better answers

Exam question: What was the purpose of Source B? Use details from the poster and your own knowledge to explain your answer.

(8 marks)

■ **A basic answer (level 1)** makes a valid comment about purpose without using detail in the source for support OR discusses valid detail in the source without linking it to the purpose of the source.

● **A good answer (level 2)** considers the purpose of the source referring to detail in the source, own knowledge or, for a more complete level 2 answer, both.

▲ **An excellent answer (level 3)** analyses the treatment or the selection of content of the source to explain how the source was used to achieve its purpose, referring to detail in the source, own knowledge or, for a more complete level 3 answer, both (for example, … *the National Government wanted to be re-elected and is implying it can solve the problems of unemployment (showing the problems as a bad thing – everyone is sad because smokeless chimneys mean unemployment). They say they are the 'remedy – the answer to unemployment but we know unemployment was still rising despite the passing of the Unemployment Act and the Special Areas Act in 1934*).

What was it like to be unemployed?

> ### Learning objectives
>
> In this chapter you will learn about:
> - experiences of the unemployed
> - evaluating the utility or reliability of sources.

In some ways, the experience of unemployment was the same for everyone. You never had enough money, so you were always making choices about spending – food or fuel or rent? You had to go to the **Employment Exchange** at least once a week, to register as looking for work ('sign on') and to collect your money – some casual workers, dock workers for example, had to sign on twice a day. All those not on NI benefit had to go through the degrading means test to prove they were poor enough for the dole. A benefit officer visited their home to find out what they possessed (if they had anything they could sell, for example). They also wanted to be told about any savings people had and any money other people in the house might have – for example, an elderly parent might have a pension or children might be earning. If their children earned even a few pence, their dole was reduced.

A British Medical Association study in 1933 showed it cost 5s 1d to feed a person the minimum of food for proper nourishment. By 1938 prices had risen and studies showed that 44% of those getting dole had to manage on less than this.

But in some ways, every unemployed person had a different experience. Were you willing to take any work, or just work at your trade? Would you spend day after day looking for work or did you, sometimes only after years of trying, give up? Did you have a family; if so, how big was it? Was your wife good at 'managing', or not? Were you happy to spend all your money on essentials – or did you spend it on beer and cigarettes? Many people joined savings clubs for necessities. They paid in a regular amount each week and then, when there was enough saved, bought the goods.

Source A	From The Road to Wigan Pier, *written by George Orwell in 1937. Orwell was a famous writer.*

Enormous groups of people, probably at least a third of the population of the industrial areas, live on the dole. The Means Test is very strictly enforced: you are refused **relief** at the slightest hint that you are getting money from another source. Dock-labourers, for instance, who are generally hired by the half-day, have to sign on at a Labour Exchange twice daily; if they fail to do so, it is assumed they have been working and their dole is reduced correspondingly…The most cruel and evil effect of the Means Test is the way in which it breaks up families. An old age pensioner, for instance, if a widower, would normally live with one or other of his children; his weekly ten shillings goes towards the household expenses…Under the Means Test, however, he counts as a 'lodger' and if he stays at home his children's dole will be docked.

Source B	*An extract from a report by one of the investigators who helped compile an enquiry into unemployment from 1936-8.*

One of the investigators visited a young couple in Liverpool, aged 26 and 23, on a bitter February afternoon. It was snowing outside. The house could hardly have been better kept and both of them were neatly dressed. Yet there was no fire, and so far that day – it was three o'clock – they had had nothing to eat. They lit the fire when he came in, for the man said "his mother had just helped them out with a bit of coal", so they could manage it. He said his wife "had something for this evening, and that they weren't starved, though sometimes they do go pretty short." It is a household like that which shows how difficult life is on the dole, however careful the housewife may be.

Alfred Smith and his family

On 21 January 1939, the weekly magazine *Picture Post* had an article about Alfred Smith – just one of the 1,800,000 unemployed. Smith lived in Peckham, in South London. He was married, with four children. They lived in four rooms (one a very small kitchen) in the basement of a house. Smith had been out of work for three years. Three mornings a week he signed on at the Peckham Employment Exchange. He spent the rest of the time looking for work. This is how the article described Smith:

His face is lined, and his cheeks are sunken, because he has no teeth. He is only 35 years old. He walks with his hands in his pockets, shoulders bent, head slightly forward. And he looks down as he walks – the typical walk of the unemployed man. He has kept his spirits through three long years of disappointment. But he is beginning to feel that perhaps there is no longer a place for him in our scheme of things – that he must change or perish.

The Smiths' budget

The Smiths got 47s 6d a week. This is their weekly budget.

	s	d
Rent	14	6
Clothing club	6	0
Insurance	1	8
Coal club	2	0
Coke (fuel)	1	0
Light	6	0
Food	16	0
Total	**47**	**2**

Old money

12 pennies (d) = 1 shilling (s)

20s = £1 (one pound)

Source C	*The Smith family sit down to dinner. Photograph from a follow-up article in* Picture Post *about the Smiths, saying that, thanks to the article in January, Mr Smith now had a job digging ditches for air raid shelters.*

Activities

1 Compare Sources A and B.

   a Write a sentence or two saying which source best shows how unemployment affected family life.

   b Explain why you chose it.

   c Write a sentence explaining what you would use the other source to show and why.

2 What would you use the information about the Smith family to show and why?

'The town that was murdered'

> **Learning objectives**
>
> In this chapter you will learn about:
> - the reasons for the Jarrow Crusade, how it was organised and opposition to it
> - making inferences from sources.

Shipbuilding in the 1930s

Shipbuilding workers suffered high levels of unemployment in the 1930s. In 1930, shipyard owners set up the National Shipbuilders' Security Ltd (NSS) to 'rationalise' the industry, making it more efficient. In practice, this meant buying up shipyards, closing them and selling off, or renting, the land. The shipbuilding areas of the north east were **eligible** for help under the Special Areas Act of 1934. But this help only reached some areas.

Jarrow

Jarrow is in Tyneside and was part of the Special Area in the north-east. Some money went to Tyneside under the Special Areas Act, but very little. Almost all the Jarrow workers worked at Palmer's shipyard, in nearby Newcastle upon Tyne. In 1934 the NSS closed Palmer's. By 1935 unemployment in Jarrow was 64%. In 1936, when some industries in Special Areas were allowed to apply for money Jarrow couldn't – there was no industry there to apply for it. By 1936 the unemployment figures improved, but by then people had been hungry for a long time – many were starving.

Hunger Marches

In 1936, the National Unemployed Workers' Movement (NUWM), a communist organisation, organised a national hunger march to London. The government opposed this, saying a government should not be pressurised into acting. People in Jarrow decided to hold their own, clearly non-political, march for work.

The Jarrow Crusade

The members of Jarrow town council, from all political parties, planned the march and marched together for some of it. They didn't use red in their banners, a colour linked to communism. They called the march 'The Jarrow Crusade' (not hunger march) and had a religious service the evening before the marchers left at which the Bishop of Durham blessed them. The marchers were 200 of the fittest of Jarrow's unemployed men – to underline that they wanted work and were fit for it, as well as being able to cope with the march itself. They took a petition signed by over 1000 people asking for work.

Opposition

The NUWM opposed the Jarrow march – saying they should join the national march. The central Labour Party and the TUC both opposed hunger marches in general (they were anti-communist, so against the NUWM) and did not change this policy for the Jarrow marchers. The Labour MP Ellen Wilkinson was told that she should not be supporting the march. She still did by pointing out that Labour and TUC policy meant that there were some towns, such as Chesterfield, where the marchers got no help from Labour or TUC members, but were fed and housed by members of the Conservative Party.

Source A	Unemployment in Jarrow 1929–36. There were about 9500 people in the workforce as a whole.		
1929	3245	**1933**	7178
1930	3643	**1934**	6462
1931	6603	**1935**	6053
1932	6793	**1936**	4065

Source B — *From a 1996 interview with Bill Batty who grew up in Jarrow and was one of the marchers.*

There was real starvation on Tyneside. It was hard for my parents – I was one of ten children. I went to school in my bare feet with big holes in my trousers. In hot or cold, in winter with six inches of snow, I'd get home and my mother had to rub a towel on my feet to stop me getting frostbite. People can't believe this, but it's true. Even when Jarrow was busy, unemployment was still high. I was one of the few to get an apprenticeship in the shipyard and one of the last apprentices to come out of the yard before it closed. I cried when the cranes came down.

Source C — *From* The Town That was Murdered, *written by Ellen Wilkinson, Labour MP for Jarrow, in 1939.*

In the early summer of 1934, it was announced that Palmer's Shipyard had been sold to the NSS. The death warrant of Palmer's was signed. The reason for Jarrow's existence vanished overnight.

73% of all those unemployed in Jarrow had been out of work for so long they no longer qualified for unemployment benefit. 43% of them had been out of work for a year – hundreds of men had had no work for five years. There was no work. No one had a job except a few railwaymen, officials, shop workers, and a few workmen who went out of the town. The plain fact is that if people have to live and bring up their children in bad houses on too little food, their resistance to disease is lowered. They die before they should.

Source D — *A photograph of the Jarrow Crusade setting off. Only men were allowed to march. The woman, Emily Robb, and her children left the march on the outskirts of Jarrow.*

Activity

In pairs, write a two-minute radio broadcast from Jarrow as the march sets out. Use Sources A–D to help you give the listeners an idea of:

- why the marchers are going to London
- who is marching
- how the march was organised
- what makes it different from other hunger marches
- what it was like when they set out (radio listeners can't see the picture).

Marching to London

Learning objectives

In this chapter you will learn about:
- the marchers; their effect on public opinion
- considering the purpose of a source
- evaluating the reliability of sources.

The marchers covered 291 miles in 22 stages. They had an old bus to carry their cooking equipment and sent people ahead to fix a place to stay and organise the cooking. They marched up to 21 miles between stops, often stopping for more than a day, so they could hold **public meetings** to explain what had happened in Jarrow and that they were asking for work, not benefits or charity.

Public reaction to the marchers varied. In some towns, the local cinemas let them in free; in Barnsley they used the **public baths** for free. Sometimes local church or council groups gave them tea and food at their stops. Sometimes they slept in halls, schools or churches; at other times they had to sleep in the **workhouse** – the last resort of the homeless and jobless.

Source A · *Part of a speech given by the Mayor of Jarrow when the marchers stopped in Ripon.*

In every town and city and village on the way to London we are going to put before the people the plight of our distressed town, so that public opinion may make itself felt. We don't want our people to be fed by charity. All we are asking is that our unemployed men be allowed to work and earn enough money to feed their wives and children.

Source B · *Bob Maugham, a marcher who had only had one month of work in ten years, remembering the meal in Leeds 60 years later.*

We got a grand meal in Leeds. Roast beef (we hadn't had that in a long time), Yorkshire pudding and a bottle of beer. Even in the Tory places we were mostly well looked after.

Source C · *The marchers being fed at a stop in Lavendon, between Bedford and Northampton.*

examzone
Top tip

Students considering the purpose of a source do well if they use the information in the caption to work out as much as possible about where the source comes from. A private diary has a different purpose from a newspaper interview. The same person may say different things about the same issue privately and publicly.

18

| Source D | Part of a speech given to the marchers by the Reverend Thomas at Northallerton. The town council had not sent anyone to greet them. |

I don't think the decision of the council not to welcome the marchers represents the feeling of the people of Northallerton. This march is the finest organised I have ever seen. It is our duty to spare no effort to help our unfortunate comrades and I think the churches of this country should have led the march and taken it right to London as an appeal not only to the Government but also to the common humanity in man.

| Source E | A painting of the Jarrow March, painted by art student Colin Moss in 1936. Moss came from a working-class background and believed in social reform. How might this have affected his painting? |

| Source F | From a book about the Jarrow Crusade written in 2005. |

Regular donations to march funds showed the level of support for the Crusade. Donations came from passing motorists, from audiences at their daily public meeting, from workplace collections and from the general public. In total the Jarrow crusade raised £1,567 0s and 5d. Of this, £680 16s 11d came from the general public. A finance committee was in charge of keeping an account of all that was taken in and spent. In all, there were four committees organising the march: roads and food; finance; publicity; and health.

examzone
Build better answers

Exam question: Use Source D and your own knowledge to explain why people supported the Jarrow March. (10 marks)

■ **A basic answer (level 1)** generalises without adequate support from source detail or own knowledge (for example, *because the marchers were unemployed*).

● **A good answer (level 2)** uses evidence from the source and/or own knowledge to support a reason.

▲ **An excellent answer (level 3)** uses evidence from the source and precise own knowledge to support a reason (for example, *We know that people did feed the marchers and give them places to stay, and let them use the public baths for free. This was common humanity, as Source D says – the marchers had so little that they got sympathy. But they also got support, he suggests, because they were well organised. D says that the march was the finest organised that the speaker had seen and we know that they had four committees to organise the march and they chose who went on the march carefully*).

Only answers that use own knowledge can reach this level.

Activities

1 Was the painter of Source E in favour of the Jarrow Crusade, against it or neutral to it? Write a sentence explaining your view, with examples from the painting.

2 a In groups, make an index card for each source. Say what it is, where it comes from and who produced it. (If it is not possible to answer all these points, write 'can't tell'.)

   b Divide the cards up according to how useful the source is in showing the following aspects of the Jarrow March:
- the feelings of the marchers
- the organisation of the marchers
- reasons for marching
- support for the marchers.

The impact of the Jarrow Crusade

> ## Learning objectives
>
> In this chapter you will learn about:
> * the effects of the Jarrow Crusade
> * evaluating a hypothesis.

Government reaction

The Jarrow Crusade reached London on Saturday 31 October. Stanley Baldwin refused to see Ellen Wilkinson (MP for Jarrow) and accept the petition. While the march was in progress the **Cabinet** (the most senior members of the government) had issued a statement disapproving of all marches, 'whatever their particular purpose'. The government made sure the marchers' benefit payments were stopped while they were on the march (leaving their families worse off than ever), because they were 'not available for work'. The Jarrow Unemployment Board offered work to one marcher, Samuel Anderson, at a shipyard near Jarrow to tempt him from the march. He didn't go. Parliament accepted the petition, but did not debate it.

Source A	A Labour Party election poster from the 1951 general election. Think about how the party is presenting itself in relation to the Jarrow Crusade.

Gains from the march?

There were some small gains. Several marchers were offered work but it meant leaving Jarrow. All but one marcher (whose sister lived in London where he was offered work as a baker) reluctantly refused. Sir John Jarvis, MP, had taken an interest in Jarrow. After the march, he said he would set up a steel works in Jarrow. His works opened in December 1937. It only employed 200 men and gave the government an excuse to ignore Jarrow.

The Jarrow legacy

Many of the marchers felt, and said, that the Crusade had failed. It did not achieve its aim. The government did not act, at once, to bring work to Jarrow. As the country rearmed in readiness for the Second World War, unemployment did drop and many Jarrow marchers found work. More than this, the Crusade became a legend, a byword for a public protest – a protest with huge public support. Support was less universal than people now believe. The political unity of the marchers did not last long either. The various political parties that came together for the march were soon opponents again. But the spirit of the marchers inspired many more modern protests.

Source B	A marcher's view, reported in the Star newspaper for 31 October 1936.

The first morning is what I'm afraid of. It'll be getting up and looking out of the window at the same old sight – Jarrow, knowing there's nothing, nothing to do. My feet hurt terribly, but, all the same, it's been a holiday. While you're marching you don't think.

Source C — *From a debate in parliament about unemployment in Jarrow and the north east in 1986. Protesters had just staged another 'Jarrow March'. The speaker was Don Dixon, MP for Jarrow.*

I vividly recall the 1936 march. As a boy of seven, I saw the marchers leave. I asked my father why they were marching. He said they were going to London to find work. I asked: 'Would it not be easier to fetch the work up here where the men are?' That same question could be asked today – fifty years later.

Last night I presented a petition on behalf of people in my constituency. There is intolerably high unemployment in Jarrow, like many other constituencies in the north, the north west, Wales and Scotland. The Government's policies are turning our areas into industrial deserts. The Government has cut regional aid. Regional aid is not charity; we do not want charity. Regional aid is a right. Central government has to care for the regions. In Jarrow, long-term unemployment has risen from 900 to 3600. I recently had a letter from a constituent, who said: 'I am still unemployed after six years. I have filled in thousands of application forms and been on hundreds of job interviews. It is slowly driving me mad.'

Source D — *From a book about the Jarrow Crusade written in 2005.*

The struggles of the 1930s had an effect on rebuilding after the war. There was unemployment provision, a regional policy, the National Health Service and government commitment to full employment.

Source E — *A cartoon about a lorry drivers' slow drive from the north east to London to protest at rising fuel prices in November 2000.*

Did you know?

In October 2011, 75 years after the Jarrow March, a group of young people marched from Jarrow to London to protest against levels of unemployment.

Activities

'The marchers might just as well not have gone on the Jarrow Crusade. They didn't get much from it and their families lost benefit while they were away.'

1 In groups, divide the sources between you. Think about how far they support the statement above.

  ● Draw a scale line that runs from 'No support' on the left to 'Complete support' on the right. Decide where to put each source on this scale and mark its letter on the scale.

  ● List the evidence from the source for your opinion.

2 Hold a debate about the statement, using the evidence from the sources and your own knowledge.

Know Zone
Unit 3B - Key Topic 1

In the Unit 3 exam you will be required to answer five questions. You have 1 hour and 15 minutes to answer all five questions, so you don't need to write huge amounts. The number of marks available for each question will help you judge how much to write. The time allocation to the right gives you a little thinking time before you put pen to paper and a few minutes to read through your answers at the end. , in question 5, you are also marked on spelling, punctuation and grammar, so make sure you leave enough time to check that at the end.

Question 1: 10 minutes
Question 2: 12 minutes
Question 3: 12 minutes
Question 4: 12 minutes
Question 5: 20 minutes

We are going to look at Questions 1 and 2. The examples of Questions 1 and 2 on these pages are based on the chapter in Key Topic 1 called 'The Impact of the Jarrow Crusade' (pages 20–21). In the exam, the sources will be provided in the sources booklet.

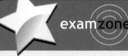

Build better answers

Question 1

Tip: Question 1 will ask you what you can learn about a particular topic from the sources provided. Be careful not just to copy information from the source. You need to make inferences from the sources – work something out based on the information in them. Let's look at an example (Source C on page 21).

'What can you learn from Source C about the impact of the Jarrow Crusade?' (6 marks)

Student answer	Comments
The source tells me that the MP making the speech saw the march as a boy and remembers it.	This answer mainly reproduces information from the source and would get very few marks.

Let's rewrite the answer, making inferences and showing how the source helped us make them.

The source tells me that the MP making the speech **saw the march as a boy and remembers it.** So <u>it must have made an impression on him.</u> Moreover, it suggests the Jarrow Crusade had enough of an impact to be <u>well known</u> – **he doesn't have to explain what it was to people and he's speaking in parliament, not in Jarrow.**	In this answer there are two inferences made from the source (<u>shown underlined</u>), using detail from the source to support the inferences (**shown in bold**). This answer would get level 3. One or two more well supported inferences would get full marks. The important thing is to make valid inferences from the source and refer to the source to show how you made those inferences. However, marks are often lost at the end of an examination by spending too much time on the first question. Make sure not to spend more than 10 minutes reading, thinking and writing your answer. Two or three well supported inferences are enough to get you full marks.

examzone
Build better answers

Question 2

Tip: The exam question will ask you to explain why a source was created – the purpose of the source. Some sources (e.g. a list of casualties in a battle) might be created just to record what happened. Others (e.g. a cartoon) might be created to get a message across and make the reader think, feel or act in a particular way. It is the second type of source you will be asked about.

The exam question will ask you to use detail from the source AND your own knowledge to explain your answer. Make sure you do both.

Study Source E and use your own knowledge. Why do you think a newspaper printed this cartoon? Use details from the cartoon and your own knowledge to explain your answer. (8 marks)

Student answer	Comments
It is making fun of the truck drivers' slow drive in 2000 comparing itself to the Jarrow Crusade. OR It shows the truck drivers are not hungry (they are eating burgers and chocolate).	Both these answers make a general statement (the first commenting on the purpose, without reference to the source, the second commenting on detail and part of the message of the source) but not explaining the purpose of the source. To improve, the answer needs tying to the question and better detail from the source AND own knowledge.

Let's rewrite the answer, making the purpose and the message of the cartoon clear (parts in **bold**) and putting it in context with our own knowledge.

The cartoon is about the truck drivers' slow drive in November 2000, protesting about rising fuel prices. The slow drive went from Tyneside to London, just as the Jarrow marchers did. But the cartoonist thinks they are exaggerating how badly off they are by making this comparison. OR The cartoon is about the truck drivers' slow drive in November 2000, protesting about rising fuel prices. But the cartoonist shows the drivers with burgers and chocolate and cigarettes and calls the Jarrow march 'the Jarrow Hunger march' (not the Jarrow Crusade, which is what it was called).	Both these answers give good detail; the first from the source, the second from own knowledge. If you put both together, it would earn a high level 2 mark. However, neither of them has analysed the information the cartoonist gives and the way he selects detail to achieve his purpose. Let's do that.
The cartoonist wants to make fun of the lorry drivers making the comparison they do with the Jarrow March. It is no accident that he has the lorry driver calling the march 'the Jarrow Hunger March', not the Jarrow Crusade (which is what it was called) while eating a burger. The cartoonist wants to say that the lorry drivers might be badly off, but not nearly so badly off as the Jarrow marchers, who had no jobs and couldn't buy much food as they went – they relied on people feeding them. His drivers are fat and they are all eating, drinking or smoking and one has a mobile - all of which costs money. If he was sympathetic to the drivers he'd show them thin and just talking, not eating and so on.	This answer discusses the purpose of the source and uses detail from the source and own knowledge to explain it. It would earn a high level 3 mark.

Key Topic 2: Britain at war 1939–1945

On 3 September 1939, Britain and France declared war on Germany, which had invaded Poland. British troops moved into France at once, but Germany did not attack until 10 May 1940. When it came, the attack was unexpectedly fast. Using the new German tactic, *Blitzkrieg* ('lightning war'), troops swept through Luxembourg, Belgium and the Netherlands into France, which surrendered on 22 June 1940. Britain was alone, but held out until the USA joined the war in 1942. The fact that Germany had attacked the Soviet Union in 1941, turning that country from an ally to an enemy, meant Germany came under attack from two sides. This increased pressure ultimately contributed to the German surrender in April 1945.

In this Key Topic, you will study:

- the BEF, Dunkirk and Churchill
- the Battle of Britain
- D-Day
- the defeat of Germany.

This book focuses on the war in Europe as it affected Britain. You will see how Britain and France were unprepared for Germany's *Blitzkrieg* tactics, how France fell and the British were forced to evacuate from Dunkirk. You will consider Churchill's role as Britain stood alone and the importance of the Battle of Britain to continuing the war. You will see how the USA and Britain landed on D-Day and how the 'drive to victory' helped to lead to the defeat of Germany.

Going to war

On 1 September 1939, the German army invaded Poland. Britain and France had been trying to avoid war with Germany by accepting Germany's breaking of the **Treaty of Versailles** and its invasion of Czechoslovakia. This policy was known as 'appeasement'. When Germany invaded Poland, it became clear appeasement was not working, so Britain and France declared war on Germany. They expected Germany to invade France over the French–German border. As soon as war broke out, the British Expeditionary Force (BEF) was sent to France. By May 1940, it had 394,165 troops defending this border. But when the German attack came, it surprised them by its speed and direction: through Luxembourg, the Netherlands and Belgium. The BEF tried to counterattack, but the direction and speed of the German attack forced it to retreat.

Winston Churchill

Winston Churchill was an MP who had constantly criticised the government's appeasement policy before the war. When war broke out, Churchill was put in charge of the navy. On 10 May 1940, when the German invasion began, he was made prime minister. He was prime minister all through the war and had a great ability to inspire people to keep going in the fight against Germany, which was particularly important once France fell.

Source A	From Churchill, *written by Martin Gilbert in 1967.*

Churchill was Britain's war leader for five years. During the first year, Britain stood utterly alone after Hitler conquered Poland, Norway, Denmark, the Netherlands and France. It was at this desperate time that Churchill raised the spirit of the British people, rallied the downhearted, gave courage to those who were afraid and persuaded the whole nation that it should resist Germany to the end, even if the end were bitter.

Exam-style question

What was the purpose of this poster (Source B)? Use details of the poster and your own knowledge to explain your answer. **(8 marks)**

Source B	*A poster issued by the British government in late 1940. The prime minister, Winston Churchill, stands in front of tanks and fighter planes. Think about the message the poster is trying to convey.*

"LET US GO FORWARD TOGETHER"

Blitzkrieg!

Learning objectives

In this chapter you will learn about:

- the German invasion of the Netherlands, Belgium and France and the retreat of the BEF
- making inferences from sources.

On 9 April 1940, Germany invaded Norway and Denmark, both neutral countries, without declaring war first. On 10 May, it launched Operation Yellow, the invasion of Western Europe. Germany's *Blitzkrieg* through Europe was a new military tactic. It followed this pattern:

- German planes bombed the area to be occupied.
- German tanks moved in and took over the area.
- German troops moved in and occupied the area, under cover of **artillery** fire.
- The planes and tanks moved on to the next target, leaving the troops to occupy the captured area and put down all resistance.

It was very risky to move into enemy territory without making sure the area behind the advancing army was safe. But it gave troops in the countries under attack little time to prepare for invasion. It was unexpected, terrifying and very effective. Belgian, British and then French troops were thrown into confusion. They tried to hold back the Germans, but had no plan, while the Germans had a very clear one. The BEF and other Allied troops were forced to retreat to **evacuate** from the French port of Dunkirk.

Source A	*From an interview with Agnis van Loon, about the invasion of Bergen op Zoom, the Netherlands, in May 1940.*

About 40 of us hid in the cellar. There was the shock of hearing German commands, heavy boots and running. We heard shots and tried to see what was going on through the grille to the street above. The Germans gathered at the crossroads, lined up in rows and marched to the town centre. The deafening sound of those marching boots, the sound of their voices singing marching songs, had a chilling effect I will never forget.

examzone
Top tip

When asked how far you agree with a statement, students who do well will always show they have thought about evidence both for and against the statement before reaching their conclusion.

Source B	*A photo of a French village that has just been captured by the Germans. The photo is from* Signal, *a German* **propaganda** *magazine.*

Source C *The effects of Blitzkrieg, 1939–40.*

Legend:
- Land occupied by the Soviet Union
- Land occupied by Germany
- Neutral countries
- German satellites
- → Allied troops evacuated
- → German invasion

Source D *From the letters and diaries of Christopher Seton-Watson, of the BEF. His company arrived in France on 5 December. Between 10 and 30 May, the company moved from France into Belgium and back to Dunkirk.*

10 May: Near Alost, we halted. There was a drone in the air, growing louder: 27 planes appeared, zig-zagging, looking for a target. We hid in the house shadows, a queer feeling in our stomachs. They passed and there were thuds not far behind us as they began bombing.

11 May: Bombing all day, waves of planes. All night the Belgian army retreated past the bombed house we slept in.

14 May: At dusk, a huge outbreak of firing told us our men were fighting German troops. We moved north – difficult over damaged roads jammed with **refugees**.

16–17 May: Much confusion with orders, but at 16:00 we were ordered to move back. It was a nightmare round Brussels. Allied army trucks and civilian vehicles kept breaking into our line. Many of our drivers had been going for so long they were falling asleep at the wheel.

27 May: At dawn, fighting with advancing German tanks, motorcycles, troop vehicles and later infantry on foot. Eventually had to pull out when came under fire from over 200 German infantry.

examzone
Build better answers

Exam question: What can you learn from Source D about the effects of *Blitzkrieg*? (6 marks)

When you are asked what you can learn from a source or sources, you are expected to make *inferences*. This means you work something out from the information in the source; you don't just copy it.

■ **A basic answer (level 1)** just repeats information from the source (for example, *it tells me that there was bombing, waves of planes and the soldiers ending up fighting the German army*).

● **A good answer (level 2)** makes unsupported inferences from the source (for example, *it tells me that things were happening very fast, it was confusing and Blitzkrieg was frightening*).

▲ **A better answer (level 3)** makes supported inferences from the source (for example, *it tells me that things were happening very fast in Blitzkrieg, because they are having to act before they get orders, it was confusing with all those refugees and the fleeing Belgian army*).

Activity

Making an *inference* is working something out from information in a source. Read the inferences below about the effects of *Blitzkrieg*. Copy each inference and write next to it the letter(s) of the source(s) that you could make this inference from. You may be able to make more than one inference from a source.

- It caused a lot of damage.
- It scared people.
- It was very successful.

Dunkirk

> ## Learning objectives
>
> In this chapter you will learn about:
> - the importance of Dunkirk
> - Churchill and the reasons for British survival
> - considering the purpose of a source.

Operation Dynamo

On 21 May 1940, the first retreating Allied troops reached Dunkirk, the only French port not held by the Germans. Its long, shallow beach would be hard to evacuate from. The British navy made plans to rescue as many troops as possible before the Germans took Dunkirk. Operation Dynamo began on 26 May. The government asked owners of small boats to go to Dunkirk to ferry soldiers to the big ships. By 29 May, about 300 boats were doing this. The big boats shuttled from Dunkirk to Britain until 4 June. They had estimated 20,000–30,000 troops might be brought home. The final total was over 338,000 – a large part of the BEF and many Allied troops as well.

The importance of Dunkirk

Many people saw the evacuation of Dunkirk as a victory, even though Winston Churchill pointed out that 'wars are not won by evacuations'. However, the evacuation saved many soldiers who could fight again and it helped British morale. Churchill knew this was important. He feared France would fall and then Britain would be the only focus of the German army and its air force, the *Luftwaffe*. So, despite his warning, he did his best to promote Dunkirk as an example of how the British people could work together to produce victory in the face of near certain defeat. 'Dunkirk spirit' became a phrase used for keeping going in the face of huge obstacles. When France did fall, the fact that the British had snatched so many troops from the overconfident Germans made people less likely to think Britain should just give in or that the Germans could never be beaten.

Source A	A painting of the last day of the evacuation of Dunkirk, commissioned by the War Artists' Advisory Committee soon after the event. The artist, Charles Crundall, was not at Dunkirk, but spoke to people who were. The details of the evacuation – the use of small ships to ferry troops, the troops massed on the beach and in the water, and the smoke of the burning oil tanks – are all accurate.

Source B *Christopher Seton-Watson was part of the BEF evacuated from Dunkirk.*

29 May: Dive-bombers came over again. Thick columns of black smoke rose from tankers burning in the harbour. Thousands of troops were waiting on the beach for orders. There seemed to be no organisation. Soldiers waded into the sea to be picked up by small boats. We decided to use the pier, where larger boats were picking up.

30 May: By 03:00, it was clear there was no hope of boarding until daylight. There was fog at first light and bombing, but the RAF kept the bombers away. There was enemy shelling, mostly at our pier. By now, embarkation was more organised. We were given number 69; 6 was just setting off. At 20:30, it was our turn and we raced through the shelling to HMS *Codrington*. We sailed at 21:30 with over a thousand aboard.

Source C *Part of the speech made by Winston Churchill on 4 June 1940.*

The Royal Navy, helped by countless ordinary seamen, embarked the Allied troops; often in bad weather, under an almost ceaseless hail of bombs and artillery fire in seas full of submarines and mines. Our men carried on, with little or no rest, for days and nights on end; trip after trip across the dangerous waters.

Our thankfulness at this escape must not blind us to the fact that this was a military disaster. We must expect another blow almost at once. We shall fight in France, we shall fight on the seas and oceans, we shall fight in the air. We shall defend our Island, whatever the cost. We shall fight on the beaches, we shall fight on the landing grounds, we shall fight in the fields and in the streets. We shall never surrender.

Source D *From the Naval Staff History of Operation Dynamo, written in 1947 using naval information from the evacuation. At first, only naval officers had access to these reports. This one was first published in 2000.*

Some delays occurred in the gathering of small craft at Ramsgate, as many had been sent to Dover in error. Once this happened, there was no way of communicating with them until they reached Dover. This resulted in delays of up to 24 hours or more before they gathered in Ramsgate. During the night, bad weather caused several collisions and vessels being cast adrift.

Exam-style question

What was the purpose of the illustration shown in Source A? Use details of the illustration and your own knowledge to explain your answer. **(8 marks)**

Activities

1 Source A was put on display in the National Gallery as soon as it was finished. Write a newspaper report by a journalist who went to the unveiling. Consider:
   - why the War Artists' Advisory Committee wanted it painted and publicly displayed
   - what the painting seems to be saying about Dunkirk.

2 Turn Churchill's speech (Source C) into four simple sentences.

3 Show how Churchill uses the following to make his speech dramatic (give one example for each):
   - repetition
   - adjectives.

4 If the navy didn't want to make the information in Source D public, why did they have the report made at all?

The Battle of Britain

Learning objectives

In this chapter you will learn about:

- the Battle of Britain
- making inferences from sources.

When France surrendered on 22 June 1940, Hitler turned to Britain. Operation Sealion (the invasion of Britain) relied on destroying the Royal Air Force (RAF) so it could not attack invading troops. The British were equally determined to win air supremacy – if not, Britain would be at the mercy of the *Luftwaffe*, and might be bombed into defeat.

What was the Battle of Britain?

The Battle of Britain was not a single battle, or even a few battles. It was the battle between the RAF and the *Luftwaffe* for control of the air over Britain, and it was fought over many months.

There were four stages to the Battle of Britain:

- **10 July–7 August:** *Luftwaffe* attacks on the British coast, especially RAF **radar** stations
- **8 August–6 September:** *Luftwaffe* attacks on RAF airfields
- **7–15 September:** *Luftwaffe*, thinking RAF beaten, attack London
- **15 September:** *Luftwaffe* defeated. This is now Battle of Britain Day, because it convinced the *Luftwaffe* that the RAF was still a fighting force. On 17 September, Hitler called off Operation Sealion.

examzone
Top tip

When asked what they can learn from a source, students who do well will make an *inference* – they will work out the implications of what the source is saying and refer to the source to support it. So, for Source A one inference would be that they had good warning of the enemy coming: they were in the air and looking for them.

Some people see 17 September as the end of the Battle of Britain. Some say (because there was still fighting over Britain afterwards) that it ended on 31 October, when the *Luftwaffe*'s focus shifted to the Soviet Union.

Why did Britain win?

In July 1940, the RAF had 640 fighter planes. The German *Luftwaffe* had 2600 bombers and fighter planes within striking distance of Britain, in occupied Europe. They were convinced that the RAF would soon be wiped out. But the RAF had some advantages. Firstly, they had radar, a system invented in 1935 and installed all along the south and east coasts of Britain at the start of the war. Radar uses radio waves to detect moving objects that the waves bounce off. It could detect the *Luftwaffe* and warn the RAF of how many planes were coming and where they were heading. Also, while the Germans had many more bomber planes, the RAF had more fighter planes and its Spitfire planes were the most efficient design. British factories worked around the clock to build more planes, and replaced lost planes much more quickly than the Germans did. Also, 'Dunkirk spirit' kept the RAF pilots flying, despite terrible losses. Once the Battle of Britain was won, Churchill said of those pilots, 'never in the field of human conflict was so much owed by so many to so few'.

Source A | *Frank Walker-Smith's flight report from his first flight on 18 August. His squadron of 13 planes fought 250* Luftwaffe *planes.*

At 17:30, I was ordered up with my squadron. Enemy spotted east of Thames estuary. I picked out an Me110. After about one-and-a-half minutes of steep turning, I attacked front on from above it, opening fire at 100–150 yards above it. I saw smoke coming from both engines as it glided down to strike the sea. After giving other enemy aircraft short bursts I delivered another frontal attack on an Me110, which broke up at about 3000 feet. The rear gunner or pilot **bailed out**. This attack took place at 5000 feet, about 60 miles due east of Margate. Only one person bailed out. Enemy casualties: two Me110s destroyed.

Key events of the Battle of Britain.

Date	Event
10 July 1940	*Luftwaffe* begins bombing attacks on British coast, especially radar stations.
12 August	*Luftwaffe* bombs British airfields and radar stations on the coast.
13 August	*Luftwaffe* bombs British airfields in Essex, Kent, Sussex and Hampshire, and aircraft factories.
15 August	*Luftwaffe* flies over 2000 raids. The day of heaviest fighting. *Luftwaffe* lost 75 planes, RAF lost 34.
16–18 August	Heavy fighting and losses.
7 September	*Luftwaffe* bombs London for the first time. The start of the **Blitz**.
7–15 September	*Luftwaffe* bombs London daily.
15 September	*Luftwaffe* runs one last bombing raid on London. They lost 60 planes (first reports put the loss as high as 185).

Source B From a book about Polish fighter pilots in Britain, written in 1998. It was Germany's invasion of Poland that started the war. Many Polish pilots escaped to fight from France and then, when France was captured, from Britain. The pilot in the extract, Boleslow Wlasnowolski, joined the RAF at Biggin Hill in early August 1940. His first flight was on 14 August.

On 13 September, Wlasnowolski moved to No 607 Squadron at Tangmere, and two days later he shot a Do17Z down into the sea. On 17 September he was posted to No 213 Squadron (which was also based at Tangmere), where he claimed his last victory on 15 October. Wlasnowolski was killed on 1 November – the day he received a posting to a Polish fighter squadron – when he was shot down.

Source C A cartoon published in a British newspaper on 19 August 1940.

"597 – 598 – 599 – 600..."

Activities

1 In groups, discuss what you can learn from the sources about pilots in the Battle of Britain. Source A has been done for you.

Source	A
It suggests...	they were well trained
because...	he knew what to do when they met the enemy, pick one and fight it, and he knew how best to do that.

2 Plan an information sheet about the Battle of Britain for Year 5 students using Sources A, B and C on these pages. You should write 200 words.

Did you know?

Hitler made a fatal decision during the Battle of Britain. Just as RAF pilot losses were becoming critical, on 5 September, the Germans reacted by shifting their sights to bombing cities rather than airfields. The extra distance involved left the German bombers undefended by their shorter-range fighter escorts. This was a key turning point in the battle, which proved a key turning point in the war.

D-Day

> ### Learning objectives
>
> In this chapter you will learn about:
> - what led up to D-Day and how it was planned
> - making inferences from sources.

On 7 December 1941, the Japanese, allies of Germany, bombed the US naval base at Pearl Harbor, Hawaii. As a result, the USA, which had been sending money and supplies to Britain, entered the war against Germany and Japan. However, the USA's main concern was the war in the Pacific, against Japan. They did not want to fight in both Europe and the Pacific for long, so made a plan for a quick invasion of Europe. The British convinced US generals that an invasion had to be carefully planned. The Germans had had years to plan their defences along the French coast. Even though troops were being moved to fight the Soviet Union in the east, there were still huge numbers in France. In August 1942, a raid on Dieppe showed the problems of trying to capture a French port from the Germans. Over 3,000 troops were killed and a destroyer was sunk. It was clear a lot of sea and air support would be needed for D-Day.

Operation Overlord

The site chosen for 'Operation Overlord' (the D-Day landings) was the Normandy coast. The **Allies** leaked information to suggest they planned to land on a different part of the French coast. The Allies realised they had to land as many troops as possible, as quickly as possible and follow up the landings with more troops and supplies. Scientists invented two floating harbours, called Mulberries, to be towed across the Channel to help land troops and equipment. Pluto, a pipeline system that could carry about a million gallons of fuel across the Channel each day, was tested and secretly laid. By the beginning of June the Allies had troops ready for the first landings on 4,000 landing craft. Over 250 warships and 11,000 planes were to support the invasion.

The first day

The day fixed for the invasion changed several times. The Allies needed good weather, enough troops at the ready in southern England and enough of the *Luftwaffe* destroyed to stop them being too great a threat to the invaders. Finally, the invasion was set for the night of 5/6 June 1944. On 5 June, various Allied and French Resistance activities suggested any invasion would be on the coast near Calais, far to the east of Normandy. Meanwhile, minesweepers cleared mines from shipping lanes all across the Channel.

In the early morning, troop landings began (see map), timed to happen at low tide on each of the beaches. Ships bombed an 80km strip of the French coast and gliders and planes began to parachute troops in. Allied planes targeted the German military defences, so they were less effective against the troops. The least successful of these attacks was on Omaha beach and this is where the losses were heaviest. Even there, the troops established a position and moved inland. The German army, under pressure on several fronts, were taken in by the deceptions and couldn't move quickly enough to stop the troops landing and establishing control of the beaches, thus allowing more reinforcements and supplies to be landed.

Source A	*From a modern dictionary of the Second World War, published in 1995.*

It became clear the invasion of Europe could not be mounted before 1944. A combined Anglo-American headquarters was set up in England in April 1943, to co-ordinate planning and, most importantly, to supervise the hugely complex and widespread deception plans being carried out by the Allies and resistance agents all over Europe.

Source B	*Landings and casualties on 6 June 1944.*

beach	troops landed	casualties
Utah	23,000	197
Omaha	34,000	2,400
Gold	25,000	400
Juno	21,400	1,200
Sword	29,000	630

Allied gains at D-Day and in the weeks that followed. Utah, Omaha, Gold, Juno and Sword were the five main landing sites of the Allied invasion.

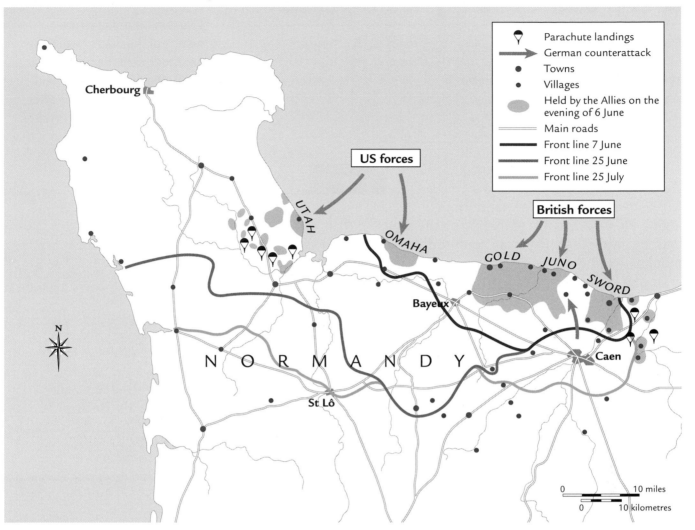

Source C	From a modern history of the Second World War, published in 1970.

Before its launch, the invasion of Normandy looked a most hazardous plan. Yet the first footholds were soon expanded into a large bridgehead 80 miles wide [an area of Allied-held land]. The enemy never managed to stop the Allies moving outwards and the whole German position in France quickly collapsed. But at the start, the line between success and failure was narrow. The ultimate triumph has obscured the fact that the Allies were in great danger at the outset and had a very close shave.

Activities

1 In groups, prepare for a debate about why D-Day was a success. Compile a list of points, making sure to use both information from the sources and your own knowledge.

2 The written sources in this chapter all come from books written after the time using many different histories and memoirs. Write a sentence or two to explain what makes such sources useful here.

Why did D-Day succeed?

Learning objectives

In this chapter you will learn about:
- the reasons for D-Day's success
- evaluating a hypothesis.

Did you know?

Winston Churchill wrote a history of the war, in which he said control of the air (won by the Battle of Britain and held by British and US planes after the USA joined the war) was vital to D-Day's success.

D-Day was a success, thanks to careful planning and preparation. It was impossible to stop the Germans seeing troops, planes and ships gathering on the coast to invade. But they were confused about where the troops would land by:

- attacks on radar stations all along the Channel and up as far as Norway
- coded radio messages and other information leaked by resistance groups and the Special Operations Executive (SOE), all suggesting the invasion would be near Calais
- a variety of complicated plans that led the Germans to believe that large numbers of troops were landing in other parts of France and that a large fleet of ships was moving towards the French coast near Calais.

Other factors

Deception was important, but Overlord needed more than that to work. The Pluto fuel pipeline, the rapid ferrying of troops and supplies once the invasion began and the air and sea backup were all vital to the actual invasion. If you look at the map on page 33 you will see that parachute troops captured inland areas on the first day. They helped the resistance to blow up railway lines and bridges and to disrupt German communications. The USA provided huge numbers of troops and a great deal of equipment, so, while losses on the first day were heavy, the Allies could keep going and keep up the pressure. The German army was under pressure in the east and in the Mediterranean (Rome was captured from the Germans on 4 June) and was not able easily to regroup and organise to fight back.

Source A — *From a history of the SOE, written in 1998.*

Two three-man teams from the SAS were dropped near the Cherbourg Peninsula to convince the Germans that the Normandy landings were only a diversion, and that the main assault was in the Pas de Calais. They were part of 'Fortitude', a deception scheme to fool the enemy into sending reinforcements to the wrong beach heads. Six SAS couldn't be mistaken for an army of invaders, so hundreds of dummies were dropped with them to give the impression of a major landing. Each team had record players to play the sound of pistol fire and soldiers' voices and had flares to light up the sky. The Germans immediately rushed troops to the area to repel the invaders and resistance workers attacked them as they went to add conviction.

Source B — *From the D-Day memories of a German soldier, published on a history website.*

There was a strong wind, thick cloud and enemy planes had not bothered us more than usual. But that night the air was full of countless planes. We thought, 'What are they demolishing tonight?' Then it started. I was at the wireless set. One message followed the other. 'Parachutists landed here, gliders reported there,' and finally 'landing craft approaching.' Some of our guns fired as best they could. In the morning, a huge naval force was seen – the last report our observation posts sent before they were overwhelmed. And it was the last report we had about the situation. It was no longer possible to get any idea of what was happening. Wireless communications were jammed, the cables cut and our officers had lost their grasp of the situation. Troops streaming back told us their position on the coast had been overrun or that the few 'bunkers' in our sector had either been shot up or blown to pieces.

Source C — From A Dictionary of the Second World War, *published in 1995.*

Perhaps the single most important factor in the success of Overlord was the deceptions, which relied on Ultra [the British cracking of German signalling codes], which enabled the Allies to monitor the German response to their deceptions and adjust their planning accordingly.

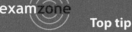

examzone

Top tip

Remember that if you are asked if a source is reliable you will always be given something to help you consider what it might be reliable for. Focus on this and remember 'reliable' means you have to think about whether or not the source is believable, not whether it is useful.

Source D — From a speech by Winston Churchill to the House of Commons on 6 June 1944.

I can state to the House that this operation is proceeding in a thoroughly satisfactory manner. Many dangers and difficulties, which at this time last night appeared extremely formidable, are behind us. We have crossed the sea with far less loss than we feared. The resistance of the batteries was greatly weakened by the bombing of the Air Force, and the superior bombardment of our ships quickly reduced their fire to a minimum. The landings of the troops on a broad front, both British and American Allied troops along the whole front, have been effective. Our troops have penetrated, in some cases, several miles inland. The outstanding feature has been the landings of airborne troops on a scale far larger than anything previously. These landings took place with extremely little loss and with great accuracy. Particular anxiety attached to them, because of problems with the light and the weather. Many things might have happened at the last minute to prevent airborne troops from playing their part. Fighting is in progress at various points. We captured various bridges which were of importance, and which were not blown up. There is even fighting proceeding in the town of Caen.

Source E — US trucks, jeeps and other supplies being ferried to Normandy a few days after the invasion began.

Activities

1. Turn the paragraph of text headed 'Other factors' on page 34 into a bulleted list of factors for success.

   a. Underline the factor supported by Source E.

   b. Circle the factor supported by Source D.

2. Use pages 32–35. List three ways that air superiority was vital to D-Day.

3. Write two or three sentences explaining how far Sources A, B, C, D and E support the following statement:

   The most important factor behind D-Day's success was the way the Germans were misled.

4. Invention was also important. Research the role played by the 'Mulberry' in D-Day.

The defeat of Germany

Learning objectives

In this chapter you will learn about:

- the reasons for Germany's defeat
- explaining causation using a source and own knowledge.

Following D-Day, Germany was under pressure from all sides (see Source A). It needed more supplies and soldiers than it could produce. The Allies put pressure on Germany by:

- bombing industrial sites, military bases and cities in Germany
- using radar to find enemy submarines and bombing them, so keeping the seas clear to ship supplies to mainland Europe
- helping resistance groups to fight the Germans and sabotage road and rail links.

The Allies still made military errors. For example at Arnhem in September 1944, they failed to liberate the Netherlands. Unlike D-Day, their plans were hurried and underestimated the German forces. Only about 2,800 of the 10,000 Allied troops involved in the attack returned.

Even so, many Germans felt Germany was going to lose. Some planned to assassinate Hitler, but the plan failed. Hitler got rid of all possible conspirators, many of whom were experienced soldiers, thus weakening his military command, and kept on fighting. In December 1944, the Germans launched a surprise attack through the Ardennes Forest in Belgium and France at the Battle of the Bulge. This time they lost, with heavy losses. By April 1945 it was clear that, under attack on two fronts and short of men, arms and supplies, Germany faced defeat. The Allies were advancing on all sides. As Soviet troops neared Berlin, Hitler committed suicide and Germany surrendered.

Source A   *Allied advances 1942–5.*

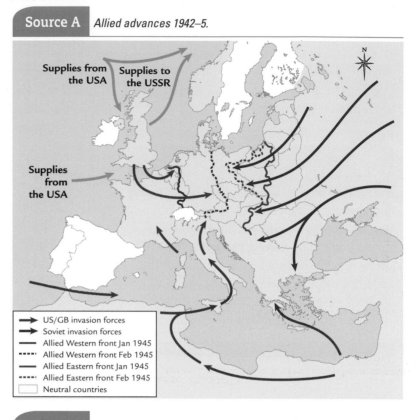

Supplies from the USA   Supplies to the USSR

Supplies from the USA

➤ US/GB invasion forces
➤ Soviet invasion forces
— Allied Western front Jan 1945
···· Allied Western front Feb 1945
— Allied Eastern front Jan 1945
···· Allied Eastern front Feb 1945
☐ Neutral countries

Source B   *From a textbook on the world since 1914, published in 1989.*

It was the massive production of the USA that made victory certain in the end. Factories in Britain and the USSR worked long and hard and produced more than seemed possible. But many of their factories had suffered war damage and they were short of raw materials and workers. In the USA there was plenty of everything and no war damage. Out of the factories poured a stream of tanks, guns, ships, trucks, planes – everything needed for war. They went not just to the US forces but to the other Allies as well.

examzone
Watch out!

The various ways of referring to Russia under communist rule can be confusing. It is sometimes called the USSR (Union of Socialist Soviet Republics) and sometimes the Soviet Union. Other people refer to it as Russia.

| Source C | A cartoon published in a British newspaper on 19 January 1945. Panzers were German tanks. It is referring to a wartime joke: 'If we only had some ham, we could make ham and eggs.' 'If we only had the eggs.' |

MODEL: "If we only had good communications we could send them our spare panzers"
RUNDSTEDT: "If we only had spare panzers"

ELASTIC DEFENCE

| Source D | Production of weaponry 1939–45 (the USA did not start production until it entered the war in December 1941). |

Country	Tanks	Aircraft	Rifles	Allied military ships or German submarines
Germany	6300	89,500	10,328,000	954
USA	99,500	192,000	12,330,000	8812
USSR	102,000	112,100	12,139,000	161
UK	29,300	94,600	2,457,000	1156

Exam question: Use Source C and your own knowledge to explain why Germany was defeated. (10 marks)

■ **A basic answer (level 1)** generalises without adequate support from source detail or own knowledge (for example, *because of the USA joining the war*).

● **A good answer (level 2)** uses evidence from the source and/or own knowledge to support a reason (for example, ... *they were short of weapons (that's why the 'no spare panzers' is in the source) and they had problems with their communications (the source shows bombed train lines*).

▲ **An excellent answer (level 3)** uses evidence from the source and precise own knowledge to support a reason (for example, ... *they were overstretched for supplies by the fighting on two fronts (that's why the 'no spare panzers' is in the source) and the Allied bombing and the work of resistance groups was ruining train lines and roads so moving troops and supplies about was much more difficult*).

Only answers that use own knowledge can reach this level.

Activities

1 Write two or three sentences to explain whether Sources A and B support the idea that the Germans lost because the Allies had more resources.

2 Design a poster using the information in Source B: 'We won the war because...'.

In the Unit 3 exam you will be required to answer five questions. You have 1 hour and 15 minutes to answer all five questions, so you don't need to write huge amounts. The number of marks available for each question will help you judge how much to write. The time allocation to the right gives you a little thinking time before you put pen to paper and a few minutes to read through your answers at the end. Remember that in question 5, you are also marked on spelling, punctuation and grammar, so make sure you leave enough time to check that at the end.

Question 1:	10 minutes
Question 2:	12 minutes
Question 3:	12 minutes
Question 4:	12 minutes
Question 5:	20 minutes

We are going to look at Question 3. We are going to focus on the chapter in Key Topic 2 called Blitzkreig! (pages 26–27).

examzone
Build better answers

Question 3

Tip: Question 3 will ask you to use both a source and your own knowledge to explain why something happened. It is testing your ability to find relevant detail and show, clearly, how it explains something.

In the exam, you cannot reach level 3 unless you use your own knowledge. Level 3 requires you to use your own knowledge very precisely. Don't be vague. Give as much useful detail as you can. *'The Luftwaffe had many more planes than the British'* is vague. *'The Luftwaffe had over 2,000 planes, the British only had hundreds'* is better. *'The British only had 640 fighter planes, the Luftwaffe had about 2,500 planes in all but that includes bombers as well as fighter planes'* is even better!

Let's look at an example.

Use Source B (on page 26) and your own knowledge to explain why *Blitzkrieg* was such an effective tactic. (10 marks)

Student answer	Comments
Source B shows a burning French village.	This answer simply describes the source. It would be a level 1 answer. To move up a level, it would need to say how the source helps you to understand why *Blitzkrieg* was effective or introduce something relevant from their own knowledge. It would score a very high level 2 mark if it did both these things. Let's re-write the answer to do that.
Source B shows a village in France just captured by the Germans, burning. The town will have been captured by Blitzkrieg, the new German tactic. You can see the effect of the bombing and the attacks by the tanks (these were the first and second stages of Blitzkrieg). You can clearly see that if an area is bombed and then attacked by tanks, one after the other, it is not going to put up much resistance once the troops move in (which was the third stage of Blitzkrieg).	This answer is much better. It uses detail from the source (the devastation from bombing and tanks) and own knowledge about how *Blitzkrieg* worked to address the question. To reach level 3 it would need to develop the argument using a deeper level of own knowledge. An answer cannot reach level 3 without using own knowledge.

Source B shows a village in France just captured by the Germans. The German army advanced through Luxembourg, Belgium, the Netherlands and France using Blitzkrieg. This was a new tactic for war. Blitzkrieg involved moving very rapidly, not stopping to consolidate victories. Before, armies had moved in and captured a place and made it secure before moving on to the next place. This was a much slower process than Blitzkrieg, but was seen as the safe thing to do. No one would expect an army to move on without making what they took secure, planning a way to retreat and making sure they would not be attacked from behind. So Blitzkrieg was successful because it was a surprise. First there was bombing by planes, then tanks moved in and took over using their heavy firepower. Finally, the troops moved in. It had the huge advantage of being so fast – the town is captured, yet it is still burning, so they moved very fast indeed. We know that when the troops reached a town the people were mainly off the streets, hiding in cellars and other places from the bombing. They will have been so scared by the bombing and the tanks that they would give in much more easily to the troops, they will have had no time to prepare.

This is an excellent answer. It would earn a high level 3 mark. It discusses why Blitzkrieg was so successful in a way that ties the information in the source and own knowledge together in a balanced analysis.

Topic 3: The Home
1939–1945

The Second World War brought war to civilians on a major scale for the first time. While soldiers fought on war fronts in various parts of the world, civilians back in Britain fought on the 'home front' – coping with bombing, the blackout, transport disruptions and shortages. Civilians also worked to support the troops – making weapons and planes, and managing supplies.

In this Key Topic, you will study:

- the Blitz
- the role of government, food supplies and rationing
- the changing role of women.

This topic focuses on the war in Europe as it affected Britain. You will consider the effects of German bombing and the preparations Britain made for this, including evacuation, the blackout, the construction of air-raid shelters and the setting-up of the Home Guard. You will also consider how the government controlled supplies and information on the Home Front by use of censorship and propaganda. You will see how the role of women changed during the war.

Government control

Learning objectives

In this chapter you will learn about:
- the threat of invasion
- the need for government control.

The war at home

As early as 1935, the government was preparing for both war and invasion. The government expected German planes to bomb Britain almost as soon as war broke out and troops to try to invade soon after. They also expected poison gas attacks. It was vital to prepare people to cope with both bombing and the threat of invasion. One of the things the government did was prepare sets of cards to go into cigarette packets that told people things such as how to protect their homes against bombing and what to do in a gas attack.

The government set up air-raid precautions and local warden to run them. People were given identity cards. Fitting stations fitted people with gas masks and explained how to use them. At first, there were not always enough gas masks to go round in the first delivery to a fitting station. Sometimes this caused real panic. People were told to carry their gas masks, their identity cards and a torch with them at all times.

The government organised **air raid shelters** and ran training on tackling emergency situations. Its first information leaflet, *Some things you should know if war should come*, reminded people about the importance of gas masks, lighting restrictions and fire precautions. It also told them the warning signals for air raids and gas attacks. Local groups practised for both air raids and gas attacks. The government set up the evacuation of children from the cities and asked for volunteers to help with that.

New ministries

If war came, the government would have to keep tighter control of Britain than before. In 1939, before the war began, the Ministry of Supply was set up to take over iron and steel production and organise war production. The Ministry of Food was another vital new ministry. The government took over vital industries and services, such as coal mining and the railways. Existing ministries were given extra powers. So the Ministry of Labour organised the armed forces and the war effort on the Home Front. One of the biggest and most important new ministries was the Ministry of Information, which controlled the information people were given and kept them informed about **rationing** and other government requirements.

| Source A | A poster issued by the Railway Executive Committee that took control of the railways during the war. |

Activity

1 List the threats to civilians in Britain the government expected and what it did to prepare.

2 What was the purpose of Source A?

3 Why might the government want control of the railways?

Preparing for war

> ## Learning objectives
>
> In this chapter you will learn about:
> - government preparation for attacks on Britain
> - making inferences from sources.

Preparing for bombing

Long before war began, the government prepared for war, certain that cities would be bombed. As early as 1935, it told local councils to build **air-raid shelters**. The Air-Raid Precautions (ARP) service was set up in 1937, with voluntary ARP wardens. By September 1939, there were over 1.5 million ARP wardens. The wardens put **sandbags** around buildings to stop bomb damage and put up huge **barrage balloons** to stop German planes flying low. They organised the '**blackout**': stopping lights showing after dark, which would show a bomber overhead that people were below. Streetlights were turned off. People covered their windows with cloth or paper. ARP wardens sounded the air-raid siren to warn of an air raid and the 'all-clear' when the raid was over. They checked that people went to shelters. Councils built a few shelters big enough to hold 50 people, but not many. The government decided not to crowd people together during bombing. Instead, from early 1939 onwards, they gave out Anderson Shelters – iron shelters to bolt together and bury in the garden.

When the bombing began, ARP wardens called the emergency services: Fire Brigade, Heavy Rescue Squads (who were trained to dig through the rubble to find survivors) and the Ambulance Service.

Preparing for invasion

On 14 May 1940, the war minister, Anthony Eden, asked for volunteers for a Local Defence Force (LDF). He expected about 150,000 volunteers; there were 250,000 on the first day. In August, the LDF, now about 1 million strong, was renamed the Home Guard. Because of the huge numbers, it took until the beginning of 1941 to give all the groups equipment and uniforms, but they began training straight away. The Home Guard manned anti-aircraft guns during air raids – the guns that tried to shoot down enemy planes. Over 1000 people were killed on this duty during the war. They helped rescue workers after air raids and cleared up the bomb damage, making roads clear first. They removed or painted over road and station signs, so the enemy would not know where they were if they landed in Britain. They put obstacles in large fields that might be used to land planes and they put barbed wire along the beaches. They were in charge of detonating or making safe unexploded bombs. Most importantly, they trained to fight a German invasion.

Source A	From a diary kept by Pat Ashford for the project, Mass Observation. This project asked people to keep daily diaries of their lives to be used as a record of the times. Think why this kind of diary might be different from a personal one.

29 August 1939: On the way home, I bought a torch and battery and looked at stuff for blackout curtains for the dining room. It would cost at least £1 to darken. I think I'll wait and see what happens.

30 August 1939: On the way home, I bought another torch and battery. I had another look at the blackout material.

1 September 1939: Our blackout curtains are now up. The whole town seems to be buying blackout paper – about every sixth person has a roll. Buses and trams are running with only headlights and the barrage balloon is up.

> ### Exam-style question
>
> **What is the purpose of the poster (Source D)? Use details of the poster and your own knowledge to explain your answer.**
>
> **(8 marks)**

Source B — *From the Mass Observation diary of Eileen Potter, who lived and worked in London. At this point, there had been no serious bombing. How do you think too many nights like this would affect people?*

25 June 1940: Woke at 1 am to the air raid siren hooting. Jump out of bed and dress in old clothes by the bed ready. I run upstairs for cushions to take to the Anderson Shelter. By the time we are ready and crossing the garden to the shelter, Mr H, the ARP warden, is looking in the back gate to see if we are alright. We settle in the shelter with cushions and rugs. I suddenly realise I am very thirsty. Brenda [her sister] went to sleep in a corner. Jack F goes out to have a look round then and Mrs F [neighbours] can't settle. If anything destroys my morale, it will be being cooped up in this shelter with such fidgety people. Brenda brought some cards to the shelter, so we try to play by torchlight, but doesn't work very well. No sound of bombing. Even I go out to wander over to the H's shelter to see how they are getting on. In the end, Mr H is just saying we might as well go back when the 'all-clear' sounds. It is dawn – might as well get up.

Source C — *From the Mass Observation diary of Edward Ward, who joined the Home Guard and was sent on several training courses.*

8 August 1940: What you are taught is not pretty. You learn how to stab a tank crew sentry in the back, so that he dies without making any noise. You are then told how to deal with the sleeping crew with nothing but a piece of lead pipe. We were told a lot about how to stop trains by filling the oil boxes with sand or grit. I learned a lot about street fighting and defending houses from a man who learned in the Spanish Civil War.

Source D — *A government poster warning people to wait for their eyes to adjust before setting off in the blackout. There were many minor accidents (such as sprained ankles) in the first few weeks of the blackout.*

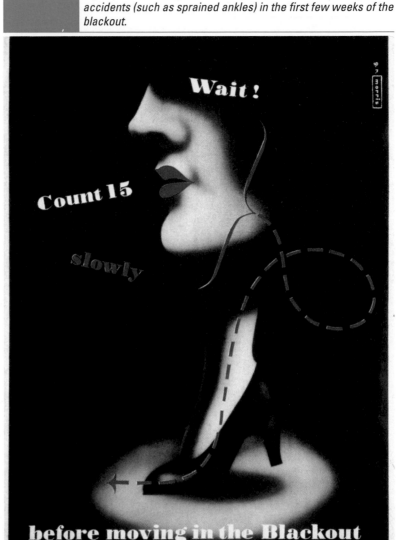

Wait!

Count 15

slowly

before moving in the Blackout

Activities

1   Making an *inference* is working something out from information in a source. Read the inferences below that can be made about preparations for war. Copy each inference and write next to it the letter(s) of the source(s) that you could make this inference from. You may be able to make more than one inference from a source.

   ● The precautions were dangerous.

   ● Some people obeyed the precautions.

   ● The precautions were a worry.

   ● The government was convinced there would be bombing and an invasion.

2   Write a sentence or two explaining what you can learn from the written sources that is not in the main information text on page 42. Give examples.

Evacuation

Learning objectives

In this chapter you will learn about:

- the evacuation of the cities
- evaluating the reliability of sources.

Did you know?

The trials of evacuees, and the clash of culture between town and city, rich and poor, are often depicted in novels set in the period: e.g. *The Chronicles of Narnia, Goodnight Mr Tom.*

At the start of the war, the government was so sure the Germans would bomb British cities, especially London, that they began evacuating people from London before declaring war. Most **evacuees** were children, but the government also evacuated some mothers of children under school age, pregnant women and blind people. This reduced the number of people in cities and it kept children (and other vulnerable groups), who would not be able to cope well with bombing, safe. It also freed parents and carers to work in volunteer groups such as the ARP or the WVS (Women's Voluntary Service).

From 1938 onwards, the government encouraged people to think about evacuation. Many people who could afford to do so made their own arrangements for evacuation with friends, family, or even strangers in the countryside.

But most ordinary children went, by train or bus, with their school. Schools practised evacuation procedure. On 1 September 1939, the evacuation began for real. In the first four days, 3 million people were evacuated, most of them children. By December, there had been no bombing. Many people went back for Christmas.

Source B	*Written in 1987 by Beryl Heard, who was ten when she was evacuated from London in 1939.*

We were given a list of things to pack. Then we were given a departure date and it came and went. Then we were given another date, and never left London. My mother was fed up with packing and unpacking, so when we were told to be ready the third time she just put a few clothes in the case [to take to school]. But we went – with about half the things we needed.

Source A	*A photo of an evacuation from London on 1 September 1939.*

Source C | From the Mass Observation diary of Eileen Potter, an evacuation officer for London County Council.

1 September 1939: Arrived at East Acton station at 7:15. The station closed to the public at about 8:15. Children from the nearest school began to arrive well before then. They marched up, all carrying kit and gas masks. Some parents came to see them off; had to say goodbye at the entrance, no room on the platform. Hardly any tears, there is a general feeling they will be back next week.

3 September 1939: Early in the afternoon had to go to Guildford with an emergency evacuation. Met up with a collection of mothers, babies and unattached children. I marched them off to the underground, helped by a 12-year-old boy who said, 'We must all pull together in these times, mustn't we, Miss?' A father, seeing my LCC armband, put two small boys in my care, saying their mother will be down tomorrow.

Source D | From a history of evacuation in the Second World War.

Getting the children out of London worked surprisingly well. The problems came on arrival. The government had left arrangements for the children's arrival and care to local authorities, telling them to do their best. The result was as a typically British wartime shamble. Hundreds of children arrived in the wrong place with not enough rations. More worryingly, there were not enough homes to put them in. A year before, the government had made lists of willing homes, but did not consider how many better-off families would make their own plans. When the trains arrived, many people on the list already had evacuees by private arrangement.

Source E | From the Mass Observation diary of Tilly Rice, pregnant mother of two, who lived near London. Tilly and the children stayed on at a Cornish home the family had rented for an August holiday.

5 December 1939: From everywhere I hear of people returning home. We have not yet decided what to do. It seems to me that they should have thought more about evacuation. The psychological effects may well be as bad as living in wartime conditions. All that money spent on evacuation could have been spent on making schools safe and building good air-raid shelters.

6 February 1940: Travelled home. Everyone is still carrying out their air-raid duties here, very good of them, considering nothing has happened now for five months.

examzone
Build better answers

Exam question: How reliable are Sources A and B as evidence of how organised evacuation was? Explain your answer using Sources A and B and your own knowledge. **(10 marks)**

■ **A basic answer (level 1)** considers a source type in general or the amount of detail (for example, *Source B is a photo it shows you a lot of children being evacuated and it looks organised*).

● **A good answer (level 2)** considers the reliability of the sources' information by referring to their own knowledge OR considers the nature/origin/purpose of the source and how it might affect reliability (for example, *Source B was written by a woman whose mother got fed up with the packing and unpacking – not all mums would have done this, so she's only evidence for her mother's level of organisation OR A is a photo of children on a station platform and they look like a whole school together, all with labels. Lots of schools were evacuated all together to the same place*).

▲ **An excellent answer (level 3)** combines both elements of level 2 (for example, *Source A could have been taken by local officials or the school or the government to show how organised things were. It does suggest things were organised. But who knows what they have in the bags? Any one of the girls could be the girl in Source B, whose mother was disorganised – and the fact she had to pack over and over, as the dates changed, suggests not everything was organised.*).

Activity

In groups, prepare to debate how far the sources support the statement below. Use all the sources and your own knowledge.

'The evacuation at the start of the war was disruptive and unnecessary.'

Blitz

Learning objectives

In this chapter you will learn about:
- reasons for the Blitz
- evaluating the reliability of sources.

The **Blitz** is the name given to the bombing of British cities by the *Luftwaffe* from 7 September 1940 to May 1941. It overlapped with the Battle of Britain (see pages 30–31). At first the raids were in daylight, but by October *Luftwaffe* losses were so great they switched to night-time bombing. The Blitz was different from previous bombing raids, which had had military and industrial targets. After the first raid on the industrial East End, the Blitz targeted civilian targets. This is because the Germans had decided that intensive bombing would wreck British morale. They believed heavy bombing, night after night, would stop people supporting the war. Then they would refuse to do war work, or follow the blackout or co-operate with the government, which would be forced to surrender.

There were bombing raids on 16 British cities, all over the country, from Glasgow to Plymouth and from Swansea to Hull. Liverpool was targeted as the most likely port for US ships bringing supplies to Britain. London was bombed first, most often and most heavily. It was bombed for 75 out of the first 76 nights of bombing (one night it was too foggy to fly).

Effects of the Blitz

The government had tried to prepare people for bombing (see pages 42–43), but they had not imagined the scale of the Blitz. Over 43,000 civilians were killed and over 2 million people were made homeless by bombing (estimates of these numbers vary very widely). Roads and railway lines were wrecked and gas, electricity and water supplies were affected.

At best, people lost a lot of sleep. A survey of Londoners for the night of 12 September 1940 showed that 32% got less than 4 hours sleep; 31% got none at all. Because the bombing was so frequent, sleep must have been this disrupted on a regular basis.

Did it work?

The Blitz certainly caused a lot of damage and destruction. It caused a second evacuation of children from the cities, splitting up families, some for a second time. Morale was weakened and some people did despair of winning the war. The Ministry of Information worked hard producing propaganda to convince people in Britain and Germany that morale had never been higher. Whether it was the work of propaganda or not, people kept going. The Blitz failed in its main objective, the British people did not turn against the war in large numbers.

examzone
Top tip

When asked to use a source and your own knowledge to explain why something happened, be sure to use both. Explain as fully as possible. So don't just say 'The Germans Blitzed the cities to harm the morale of civilians'. Add to this, 'to turn them against the war and put pressure the government to surrender'.

Source A	*From an article for the US* New Yorker *magazine, written by Mollie Panter-Downes, an American who lived in London during the war.*

14 September 1940
Hardly anyone has slept at all in the past week. The *Blitzkrieg* continues to be directed against such military objectives as the tired shop girl, the red-eyed clerk, and the thousands of weary families patiently wheeling their few belongings in prams away from the wreckage of their homes. The amazing part of it is the cheerfulness and strength with which people do their jobs under nerve-wracking conditions. Girls have taken twice as long to get to work and look worn when they arrive, but their faces are nicely made up and they bring you a cup of tea or sell you a hat as chirpily as ever.

Source B | *From the Mass Observation diary of Christopher Tomalin, a 28-year-old who lived with his parents in London, 15 September 1940.*

We can't afford to buy stuff for a 'refuge room'. We have no Anderson Shelter. We must use the pantry under the stairs: one wall is an outside wall; the other is thin board. I am scared by the indiscriminate night bombing of London and the rest of England. It is obvious the RAF and the anti-aircraft people can't do much about it. We can beat them in daylight, but not when it's dark. How can I, or anyone, sleep under these conditions?

Source C | *From the Mass Observation diary of Pam Ashford, who lived in London, 15 September 1940.*

Earlier this week, I said that people did not seem to be taking the idea of invasion seriously enough. They do now. No one doubts that we'll win. The sooner they come, the sooner they will be defeated. Hatred against the Germans is now intense – parachutists and seaborne invaders would get badly beaten up.

Source D | *A photo taken during the Blitz on London. Not many colour photos were taken at the time, as the film and processing were difficult and expensive.*

examzone
Top tip

When asked about how useful a source is for a particular purpose, students need to do more than give a general comment about its usefulness (for example, *because the person was there at the time*). They need to consider how useful the source is for the particular purpose, using detail from the source. They also need to consider how typical or reliable the sources are.

Activities

The British government worked hard to convince the Germans that British morale was high during the Blitz.

1 Write down which source you think best shows the effects of the Blitz and explain why you chose it.

2 Write down which source you think the Nazis would want to use in 1940 to show public reaction to the Blitz. Explain why you chose it.

3 Now do the same for the source you think the British government would want to use in 1940 to show public reaction to the Blitz.

Blitz on Coventry

> ### Learning objectives
>
> In this chapter you will learn about:
> - the Blitz on Coventry
> - considering the purpose of a source.

After the London Blitz, the RAF bombed German cities too. Civilians on both sides were 'getting it' – as the British often referred to the bombing. On 8 November 1940, the RAF bombed Munich. The *Luftwaffe* bombed Coventry in retaliation, in a raid so destructive that a new word came into use: 'coventration' – wiping something out completely.

The bombing began at 7:20 pm on 14 November. Bombs were dropped in the city centre to start fires to guide later bombers. Hours later, the city was burning so fiercely that it was visible from 150 miles away. The bombing went on all night – 500 bombers dropped thousands of bombs. The 'all-clear' did not go until 6:15 the next morning. Estimates of those killed range from 380 to 554 and there were thousands of injuries. Over 4000 homes were destroyed as well as factories, businesses and the city's cathedral. The *Luftwaffe* returned to Coventry 40 times, the last raid being in August 1942, but the first raid was by far the worst.

Source B — *Ted Simmonds lived in Coventry, repairing various large machines for food preparation. This is part of an account compiled by his daughter from his handwritten recollections.*

The morning after the Blitz, council officials came to ask him for help. Thousands of homeless people were wandering the city. All gas and water mains were disrupted.

The most urgent need was to give people hot tea and maybe some bread. The officials had sent men to map the broken mains to find the best routes for repairs to the Technical College (the only large building still standing in the town centre) and the bakeries.

Could Ted suggest a way to provide a lot of hot water? And could he get some food preparation machinery into the College, so they could get on with more substantial supplies of emergency food?

Source A — *A photo of Coventry taken on 9 December 1940.*

Did you know?

Films of the Blitz, on Coventry and other British cities, were shown in US cinema newsreels all over the USA as part of the US government's propaganda to get people to accept the USA joining the war.

Source C *Part of an article in the* Guardian *newspaper for 16 November 1940.*

The famous Cathedral is little more than a skeleton, masses of rubble piled inside its bare walls, while other targets included two hospitals, two churches, hotels, clubs, cinemas, public shelters, public baths, police station, and post office. The Mayor (Alderman J. A. Moseley) also gave the assurance that 'everything possible will be done for the sufferers and the homeless'. Mobile canteens are doing magnificent work in helping to feed the homeless people, and this evening private cars, loaded to capacity with comforts were pouring into the city.

Within a few hours of the raid, Mr Herbert Morrison, Minister of Home Security, was on the scene. Mr Morrison said: 'The National Service units of the city have done their duty magnificently. They have shown great courage and determination under exceptional strain. I am very grateful to them for their devotion to duty. The local authority is taking full and prompt measures to deal with the emergency.'

exam zone

Watch out!

When asked about the *purpose* of a source, do not confuse 'message' with 'purpose'. The purpose of a source is the effect the person who produced it wants it to have. The message of Source D could be 'we are coping'. The purpose of the photo was probably to raise morale.

Source D *A photo taken in Coventry after heavy bombing on 10 April 1941.*

Activities

1 In pairs, discuss why you think Source A was taken. Think of two good reasons for your answer.

2 In pairs, read Source C.

   a Write down four words or phrases you think show the writer wanted the reader to think well of the people of Coventry.

   b Write down a sentence you think shows the writer wanted the reader to think badly of the Germans.

   c Write a one-sentence slogan to convey the message of Source C.

   d Write a sentence describing the purpose of Source C.

New dangers

Learning objectives

In this chapter you will learn about:

- how German bombing changed and developed after the Blitz
- explaining causation using a source and own knowledge
- considering the purpose of a source.

More bombing

The end of the Blitz ended the heavy bombing of target cities, but the *Luftwaffe* still bombed Britain. There were many other raids – smaller, but still devastating for the bombed places. In April 1942, the Germans planned raids on new targets, smaller towns of no military importance. These are often called *Baedeker* raids because the Germans were said to have chosen their targets from towns with three stars in the German *Baedeker* tourist guide to Britain. The big *Baedeker* raids in April were on Exeter, Bath, York and Norwich. In June, the *Luftwaffe* bombed Canterbury after the RAF bombed Cologne. While the raids caused a lot of damage, the *Luftwaffe* suffered heavy losses. They had even heavier losses in the last big raids, in January 1943. They lost a bomber and four trained crew for every five civilians killed.

New bombs

So the Germans looked for ways to bomb Britain from a distance. German scientists had developed a flying bomb called *Vergeltung* ('retribution'), V1 for short. V1s were driven by a motor that was supposed to cut out over the target. They were launched from the French coast. The first V1s were launched on 12 June 1944. Over 9000 V1s were launched; many failed to reach their targets and some failed to explode. They killed about 6000 people and did cause panic at first – about 1.5 million people left London. In September, the V2 was used. It was rocket-powered, so was faster and could go higher, although it only had the same amount of explosive, so caused no more damage than the V1 when it exploded. Over 5000 were launched, but only about 1000 reached Britain, killing about 2700 people.

Source A	*A cartoon published in a British newspaper on 19 June 1944. Think about the message of the cartoon and the purpose of the cartoonist in drawing it.*

"GOOD HEAVENS, WE CAN'T WIN A WAR THIS WAY!"

Source B	*From the Mass Observation diary of Maggie Joy Blunt, who lived in Slough, for 25 June 1944.*

The first day they came over, we were told to go to the shelters. I took one look at them and fled. N says they have had a demoralising effect in London – to hear them coming and not know where they will fall. There is no defensive gunfire as a warning. She says she prefers the ordinary Blitz and has had very little sleep recently. She has even sent me a copy of her will to keep safe. Have been told that there are only enough of these bombs to last a fortnight, but that then they will be replaced by some other Secret Weapon.

Source C — Some 1944 entries from the Mass Observation diary of Edward Stebbing, who worked in a North London hospital.

19 June: Talk about the pilotless planes is endless. It seems they travel too fast and too low for radar or the anti-aircraft guns to catch them. I must admit these things have put my nerves on edge more than ordinary raids. I suppose it is because they are new and so devilishly clever.

22 June: I went to look at the destruction caused by a P-plane that fell in Tottenham Court Road three days ago. I was surprised that the really bad damage seemed confined to quite a small area.

26 June: The baker told my landlady he didn't bake enough bread for everyone today – they had to keep stopping work for the flying bombs.

27 June: I heard one of the flying bombs for the first time last night – I hope it will be the last. It seemed to come low over the houses, making the house vibrate with the noise then the engine suddenly stopped and I thought our last hour had come.

Source D — From the memories of Ivy Gross, interviewed about her wartime experiences in 1970.

I never left London all through the war. In the Blitz, you had warning and time to get to shelters. I had the round of an insurance salesman who went off to fight. So I was out on my bike every day, visiting the people on my round, collecting money, having a cup of tea. We didn't like the V1s ('doodlebugs' we called them, because of the engine noise) because you knew if you could hear the engine cutting out the blast would be near you. I was blown off my bike once. But the V2s were the worst. You didn't hear them coming – just the bang as they exploded. I don't think we could have held out with them coming over for too many months.

Source E — A photo taken after one of the last V2s hit Smithfield, London on 25 April 1945. The government stopped the publication of the photo. Why do you think they did this?

Activities

1 Write a paragraph explaining how far Sources B, C and D agree about the effect of the V1 and V2 bombs on morale.

2 Write a paragraph explaining how far Sources A and E agree about the effect of the V1 and V2 bombs on morale.

3 Write a sentence explaining the message of Source A.

4 Look at Source E.

   a Write a note from the photographer to his newspaper, explaining why he took the photo.

   b Write a note from the government to his newspaper, explaining why they can't print it.

The Ministry of Information

Learning objectives

In this chapter you will learn about:

- the use of censorship and propaganda
- evaluating the reliability of sources.

Censorship

The most important Ministry of Information (MOI) work was propaganda and **censorship**. Censorship is stopping the passing on of certain information – in newspapers, radio broadcasts, private letters and even conversations. The aim was to stop information getting out that would encourage the enemy and demoralise the British people. Censors told newspapers and magazines what information and pictures they could (or could not) print. They censored letters going abroad and coming into the country to make sure that important information was not given away. The armed services had their own censors to go through the troops' mail.

Propaganda

Propaganda is giving people information in order to make them think or behave in a particular way. The MOI had been impressed by the Nazis' use of propaganda in the 1930s. It quickly built up a large team of workers to produce posters and leaflets to persuade people to do (and not to do) certain things to help the war effort. It also made 'how to...' films showing people, for example, how to move around safely in the blackout or how to dig a vegetable plot. There were also patriotic short films and newsreels about the war, such as *Britain Can Take It*. These were shown at the cinema and MOI vans toured the country showing these films in town and village halls. There were also talks on the radio. The censors made sure that feature films made during the war, such as *The Lion has Wings* and *Henry V*, encouraged patriotic feeling.

Source A

From a newspaper article on the autobiography of Ruth Ive, who was a telephone censor in the war. The telephone cables across the Atlantic had been closed down, but there was one 'hotline' in use.

Before a caller was connected, even the King, Ruth had to read aloud this warning: 'The enemy is recording your conversation and will compare it with previous information in his possession. Great discretion is necessary. Any indiscretion will be reported by the Censor to the highest authority.' Once she had to pull the plug on Churchill. He had booked a call to Anthony Eden, who was visiting Canada after a V2 rocket attack in Smithfield [Source E, page 41], with dozens of casualties.

After greeting Eden, Churchill began, 'This morning at 12:00...'. Ive made a split-second judgment, reached for the off switch and warned: 'I must remind you, sir, that there should be no mention of any damage suffered from enemy aircraft. Would you like your call reconnected?' She did this, but Churchill began again, 'Anthony, this morning...'. Ive recalls: 'He sounded so upset, but I had no option but to disconnect him again and warn him of the dangers.'

Source B

The censor's office, Liverpool, in November 1939, two months after war was declared. At this time, there were 1300 censors working on letters and telegrams.

Source C *From a government leaflet on how to 'make do and mend', published during the war.*

There are a wealth of ideas for letting out children's clothes [undoing the stitches and making the seams smaller to make the garment bigger]. An outgrown dress should be completely unpicked from hem to underarms and then along the sleeve seams, so it can be opened flat in one piece. Contrasting bands of material can then be let in at the sides, waist, across the shoulders and along the sleeves if needed.

Source D *Poster produced by the Ministry of Information in 1940.*

Source E *Poster produced by the Ministry of Information in 1940.*

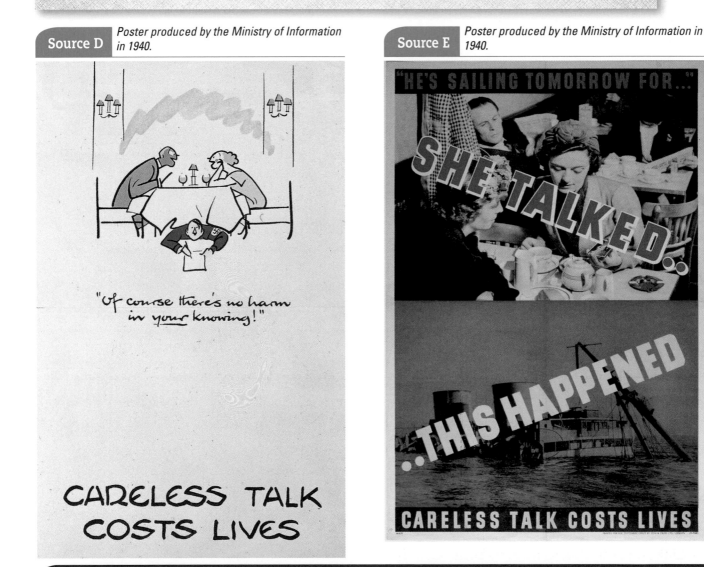

Activities

1 Study Source D. Hitler never came to Britain during the war so was never under a restaurant table taking notes on what people said. Does this mean the source is not reliable for a historian? Write a short paragraph to explain your answer.

2 Copy and complete the table below.

Source	A	B	C	D	E
Most useful for…	the extent of censorship				
because…	even Winston Churchill was censored!				

3 How do Sources D and E show how important propaganda was during the war?

Rigationing

> ## Learning objectives
>
> In this chapter you will learn about:
> - the impact of the war on the food supply and how the government dealt with it
> - making inferences from sources.

Before the war, Britain **imported** 55 million tons of food a year – 70% of all the food people bought. The Ministry of Food began planning to control the food supply in November 1936, fearing the Germans would sink ships supplying Britain. They were right. By January 1940, German submarines had sunk over 100 ships carrying food to Britain.

Rationing began on 8 January 1940. What was 'on the ration' and the rationed amount changed during the war. People had ration books of coupons. They registered with a shop and the shopkeeper recorded the coupons used. There were three kinds of rationing:

- rationing of foods such as butter by weight
- rationing of dried goods (e.g. flour, biscuits, cereal) and tinned goods on a point system (goods were worth a varying number of points; there was a weekly point maximum)
- government control of foods such as orange juice or milk, where babies, pregnant women or the sick were given supplies first.

The Ministry of Food encouraged people to grow their own food and keep chickens and rabbits. Local parks were turned into allotments to grow crops on. Even the moat around the Tower of London was dug and planted. Many people joined 'pig clubs': buying a pig, sharing its care then sharing the meat when it was killed. But even so, food was scarce and there was little variety. Ministry of Food broadcasts gave recipes and tips for making food go further. People swapped food with their neighbours and shopkeepers favoured regular customers. A 'black market' grew up where you could buy rationed or scarce goods at high prices. The government punished black marketeers and their customers, but it still flourished, especially in cities where people were less able to grow their own food.

Source A	*The average ration for a person for a week in 1941.*

2 oz (56 g) butter
4 oz (113 g) cooking fat
1 oz (28 g) cheese
2 oz (56 g) tea OR coffee
2 oz (56 g) jam or other preserve
4 oz (113 g) bacon or ham
8 oz (226 g) sugar
1 shilling-worth of meat. This bought about 12 oz (340 g) of stewing beef, more of mince, less of steak
1 egg
2 pints (1.1 litres) milk

Source B	*The 'official' recipe for Woolton Pie, from* The Times, *26 April 1941.*

In hotels, restaurants and communal canteens, people have tasted Lord Woolton Pie and found it good. Like many economical dishes, it is good for you and provides necessary vitamins. The ingredients can be varied according to the vegetables in season. Here is the official recipe:

Take 1 lb (500 g) each of potatoes, cauliflower, swede and carrots, 3 or 4 spring onions (if available) 1 teaspoon of vegetable extract and 1 tablespoon of oatmeal. Cook for 10 minutes with just enough water to cover. Stir occasionally, to prevent sticking. Allow to cool. Put into a pie dish, sprinkle with fresh parsley (if available) and cover with a lid of mashed potato or wholemeal pastry. Bake in a hot oven until topping is nicely browned and serve hot with brown gravy.

Source: The Times, 26 April 1941, © The Times/NI Syndication Ltd. 1941.

Source C	Extracts from the diaries of Clara Milburn, who lived near Coventry during the war.

8 July 1940: Lord Woolton spoke on the radio. Without warning tea, margarine and cooking fats are to be rationed.

31 December 1940: Lord Woolton asked us to 'go carefully with the tin opener'. Potatoes and oatmeal are plentiful, but we must eat less. He does not want to ration cheese, but asks us to leave it for vegetarians and workers.

7 January 1941: Lord Woolton says the 1s 6d meat ration may have to go down to 1s 3d.

13 February 1941: conversation in Malin's [the greengrocers]: 'Any oranges?' 'What a thing to ask, madam, considering the sign on the door!' Mr Malin (interrupting) 'Finch, get Mrs Milburn half a dozen.' The sign said 'No Oranges'.

5 December 1941: Got 5 lbs of apples at the greengrocer. Mrs Malin treats me very kindly – she let me have 3 lbs of potatoes the other day; for regular customers only.

21 September 1942: Saw Mrs Greenslade in town and swapped some pears and apples for a chicken.

Source D	A Ministry of Food wartime poster.

Activities

1 Work in pairs.
   a List the things you can learn about rationing from the sources.
   b Underline things said by more than one source.

2 Read Source B.
   a Write a description of what you expect Woolton Pie would be like to eat.
   b List the benefits of the pie, from Lord Woolton's point of view.

3 Research the impact of rationing and the war on non-food products, e.g. fuel and luxury goods.

examzone
Build better answers

Exam question: What can you learn from Source D about food during the war? (6 marks)

When you are asked what you can learn from a source or sources, you are expected to make *inferences*. This means you work something out from the information in the source; you don't just copy it.

■ **A basic answer (level 1)** just copies the information (for example, *It tells me they told you not to waste food*).

● **A good answer (level 2)** makes unsupported inferences from the sources (for example, *they must have been short of food*).

▲ **A better answer (level 3)** makes supported inferences (for example, *the government was saying it was important not to waste food, so important that wasting it could mean Hitler would win the war. This probably means it was in short supply*).

Working women

> ### Learning objectives
>
> In this chapter you will learn about:
> - the war work women did
> - explaining causation using a source and own knowledge.

As with the First World War, the Second World War took huge numbers of men into the armed services. At first, large numbers of unemployed men took over their jobs. But the government re-formed the Women's Land Army in July 1939. It knew that it would need to clear and farm more land to produce the huge amounts of food the country would need when war began. It was right. By March 1940, over 30,000 men had left farming for the army and over 15,000 had left to do other war work. It quickly became clear that women were needed for all types of war work.

Heavy industry

Women also worked in engineering firms, iron foundries and factories. Many women were nervous of the huge machinery at first, as well as what one woman called 'the all-male feel of the place'. Usually they were supervised by a man. Once they learned what to do and grew in confidence, many women took to the work and enjoyed it. Those who did well were often respected, although some men never changed their view that women shouldn't do this work, and some women did find the work too difficult.

Conscription

On 8 December 1941, the government introduced **conscription** for all unmarried women aged 20–30. As the war went on, older single women and then married women were also conscripted. Women could choose to join the armed services, civil defence or industry. They joined all of these in large numbers and were soon doing vital work – by 1943 there were over 100,000 women working on the railways, doing every kind of job from selling tickets to driving the trains.

In the services

Women had their own sections in the armed services: the ATS (army), the WAAF (air force) and the WRNS (navy). At first, their work was almost entirely cleaning, cooking or office work – the war created huge amounts of paperwork. They were also trained as drivers. Women could not go into battle but, as the war progressed, they worked on anti-aircraft posts, as radio operators, as motorbike messengers and even as spies.

Source A	*Women bus drivers in Bournemouth learning how to maintain an engine on 14 November 1941.*

Source B | *From* Instructions for American Servicemen in Britain, *a booklet issued by the US War Office for soldiers going to fight in Britain in 1942.*

British women officers have stuck to their posts near burning ammunition dumps. They have delivered messages on foot after being blown off their motorcycles. They've pulled airmen from burning planes. They've died at gun posts and, as they fell, another girl has stepped up and carried on. They've won the right to the utmost respect. When you see a girl in uniform with a ribbon on the tunic, remember she didn't get it for knitting more socks than anyone else in Ipswich.

Did you know?

The government recognised the importance of childcare for working women. They set up nurseries and encouraged job sharing between women with children to allow mothers to work.

Source C | *From a book written about the Special Operations Executive (SOE) in 1999. The author is writing about F section, which sent 470 people to France altogether.*

The SOE was unusual in that it treated women on a perfect equality with men. For their purposes, there were several jobs that women performed better than men. The French [F] Section sent 39 women to France on missions with the French Resistance, 13 died there. The usual SOE groups consisted of an organiser – usually a man; a courier to take messages – usually a woman; a wireless operator – a man or a woman and a sabotage instructor – always a man.

Source D | *Women maintaining a spitfire plane for the RAF, photographed in 1942.*

Exam-style question

What was the purpose of Source C? Use details of the source and your own knowledge to explain your answer. (8 marks)

Activities

1 Write a sentence explaining how Source C contradicts itself about the position of women in the SOE.

2 Read Source B. Write a circular for British women officers explaining the problems they might have with US servicemen.

3 How far do Sources A, B, C and D agree that women were treated equally at work in wartime?

Working after the war

When the war came to an end there was a sudden change to work and the workforce. Millions of men and women were discharged from the services and needed to find civilian jobs. Women who had been 'minding' jobs for servicemen had to give them up when these men came home. Women had to leave the services and war work, too. But women had now tasted the independence that having their own income provided. While attitudes to women working, especially married women, did change because of the war, it was seen as most important to find men work.

Source A *An aircraft factory photographed in January 1930.*

Source B *Statistics of women as part of the workforce for 1931 and 1951, from the Census (all figures in thousands).*

	1931	1951	increase
Women in the workforce	6265	6561	5%
Total workforce (men and women)	21,054	22,210	5%
All women of working age	18,321	20,045	9%
Women as a percentage of the workforce	30%	30%	
Women in the workforce as a percentage of all women of working age	34%	33%	

Source C *Barbara Davies worked at an aircraft factory in Coventry during the war. After the war, she and all the other women in the factory were told they had to leave.*

I went on the night shift one night and was told I was no longer needed. As you can imagine, I wasn't pleased. We went straight round to the trade union representative. He said that the jobs were for the men coming out of the forces; that we had to leave the jobs for them. There was nothing we could do at all.

58

Source D
From a history of Britain written in 1987.

In 1911, women made up 30% of all non-manual workers. Of nurses and teachers, 63% were women. By 1951, there were two other types of employment in which women were in the majority – clerks (60%) and shop workers (52%). The public were often felt to prefer women to men in these jobs. They were also the jobs in which casual work and low pay were common and women were not seen as posing a threat to the career prospects of men.

Source E
An aircraft factory photographed in March 1951.

examzone
Build better answers

Exam question: Source C suggests that, after the war, women were expected to just be housewives again. How far do you agree with this interpretation? Use Sources B, C and D, your own knowledge and any other sources you find useful to explain the answer. **(16 marks)**

■ **A basic answer (level 1)** generalises without support from source detail or own knowledge.

● **A good answer (level 2)** makes a judgement, using support from the sources and/or own knowledge. A more complete level 2 answer considers evidence for or against the view. (for example, *B seems to support C as it doesn't show a huge increase from the pre-war figures for women working. But then if you look at the two plane factory pictures you can see that in 1930 the workers were all men and in Source E there is a woman although you can only see two workers. Also, Source D seems to suggest the range of work for women grew*).

▲ **An excellent answer (level 4)** focuses on the question, evaluates the evidence for and against it, from sources and own knowledge and reaches a judgement. (for example, … *The statistics (B) suggest that there weren't that many more women working – which would support Source C where the woman in the aircraft factory really didn't want to leave, but was forced out. But then Sources A and E are also aircraft factories and they suggest it went from all-male to having at least some women workers. So not all sources support the suggestion in B. Source D suggests that there was more work for women after the war, but in 'suitable' jobs, not where they took jobs from men. However, we have to consider that the women were under pressure. It wasn't just that married women had home lives to get back to (if their husbands came home and their children back from evacuation). It is also that it would be seen as patriotic to make way for the returning men.*

Make sure you write accurately when answering these questions – there are 3 extra marks available for spelling, grammar and punctuation.

Activities

1 Write a short newspaper report headed: Working women 1931–51: change or continuity? Use the statistics in Source B.

2 In groups, prepare to debate the statement below, using the sources as evidence.
   Women had greater job opportunities after the Second World War than before it.

60 In the Unit 3 exam you will be required to answer five questions. You have 1 hour and 15 minutes to answer all five questions, so you don't need to write huge amounts. The number of marks available for each question will help you judge how much to write. The time allocation to the right gives you a little thinking time before you put pen to paper and a few minutes to read through your answers at the end. Remember that in question 5, you are also marked on spelling, punctuation and grammar, so make sure you leave enough time to check that at the end.

Question 1:	10 minutes
Question 2:	12 minutes
Question 3:	12 minutes
Question 4:	12 minutes
Question 5:	20 minutes

Here, we are going to look at Question 4. The question below is based on the chapter in Key Topic 3 called 'The Ministry of Information' (on pages 52–53).

examzone
Build better answers

Question 4

Tip: Question 4 will ask you to consider the reliability (accuracy) of two sources. You will need to use detail from both of the sources and your own knowledge to answer the question.

In the exam, you have to do two things to reach the top level. You need to evaluate the reliability of both sources by considering the information they provide and weighing it against your own knowledge. You also need to consider the nature/origin/purpose of the sources. Only then, having weighed these up, should you reach your judgement.

Let's look at an example.

How reliable are Sources D and E (on page 35) as evidence of the success of D-Day? Explain your answer using Sources D and E and your own knowledge. (10 marks)

Student answer	Comments
Source D is good for their success, it tells you all the things they did.	This answer judges reliability on the amount of detail in the source. It is a good level 1 answer. Other possible level 1 answers are those that judge reliability by source type (for example, *it's a speech, it must be unreliable*) or subject (for example, *it's all about the success of D-Day*). To reach level 2 the answer would have to EITHER: evaluate the information in the source by testing it against own knowledge for reliability, OR: evaluate the nature/origin/purpose of the source by testing it against own knowledge for reliability.

examzone

Build better answers

Let's rewrite the answer with some more thought given to the information in the sources.

Source E is a photo of the US equipment being ferried across the Channel for D-Day. You can see quite a lot of equipment, and this is just one landing craft and we know there were thousands of landing craft for troops and equipment. We know that two of the big reasons for the success of D-Day was that it was planned to get troops and equipment across quickly and all the supplies and troops the Allies had from the USA.
OR
Source D is a speech made by Churchill after D-Day to the House of Commons. It is certainly suggesting that D-Day was a success. If you believed everything it said, then you would think it was excellent evidence for the success of D-Day – all those details of what was done. However, you have to consider that this was a speech by Churchill. He would want to make D-Day seem as successful as possible. Not only so that the House of Commons would be reassured, but also all the British people who read the reports. He'd also want the Germans to read his speech and be convinced by it. On the other hand, he couldn't lie completely and Source E seems to show part of a large scale landing force (as he says) – we know there were thousands of landing craft.

These answers are much better. They are level 2 answers. They consider the source(s), not just types of source and they also both use own knowledge to support their answer. The key thing is that they explain why they have made their decision. It's OK to say you don't know if a source is reliable – but you have to explain why you don't know.
A more complete level 2 answer will evaluate both sources, not just one of them. The second answer does this. To reach level 3, an answer would need to do both parts of level 2. Let's do that.

Let's rewrite the answer, adding the analysis.

Both sources suggest D-Day was a success and I think they are pretty reliable evidence. Source D is a speech by Churchill. So you have to consider that he will be making the best of D-Day for propaganda reasons – he'd want to convince both sides that it had been a success by this point in the first day (so the British feel encouraged and the Germans discouraged). We know troops were parachuted in and he talks about these and the landing of British and US troops on a broad front. Maybe he exaggerates the success, with phrases like 'fewer losses than we feared', 'landings took place with extremely little loss and with great accuracy'.
As for Source E, it shows a lot of jeeps and supplies being landed and we know there were thousands of landing craft and that the USA provided a lot of supplies and troops and that these things contributed to the success of D-Day. We don't know what happened to these supplies, though – the photo is just evidence that there were a lot of supplies.

This is an excellent answer. It discusses the reliability of both sources in a way that ties the information in the source and own knowledge together in a balanced analysis.

Key Topic 4: Labour in power 1945-51

Once the Second World War had ended, the British government faced many difficult tasks. In Europe, British politicians and the British army had to take part in the political settlement, while British aid organisations helped the millions of refugees who had been displaced by the war. Back in Britain, there were many problems caused by the war, which the government also had to deal with. These included a huge war debt to the USA, which made the government reluctant to commit to spending on welfare.

In this Key Topic, you will study:

- Labour comes to power
- responding to Beveridge: the attack on 'want'
- the NHS.

You will see how the 1945 General Election campaign progressed, how and why the Labour Party won and how it identified the most pressing social problems of the time and set out to solve them. You will consider the many difficulties it faced in doing this, including opposition to its plans from those who were asked to put them into practice – for example the opposition of many doctors to the idea of a National Health Service.

Labour comes to power

Many people in Britain saw May 1945 as the end of the war, even though the Allies were still fighting Japan. Hitler was beaten, the threat of bombing had been lifted and people began to look to the future. Rationing was worse and the bombing had made many people homeless. There were still shortages as factories and farms switched to peace-time production. People wanted homes, jobs and a chance for a better life. But which government would provide this?

Calling an election

Churchill (Conservative leader; prime minister) and Attlee (Labour leader; Churchill's deputy when he was abroad) both wanted to keep the coalition government going until Japan was beaten. The Labour Party and the Liberals wanted an election at once. Many Conservatives also wanted an election close to the end of the war in Europe. They felt they would get votes from the popularity of Churchill's war leadership. The government gave way under all this pressure and on 23 May 1945, Churchill resigned and an election date was set for 5 July.

The main contenders in the election were the Conservative and Labour parties. They chose very different strategies. The Conservatives focused on Churchill and the war – not the party or the future. One of their slogans was 'Let him Finish the Job'. Labour, on the other hand, focused on the future. They promised reform. They also built on the desire for social change that the war had produced. Many people felt they had fought hard for a better, fairer society.

Source A *From the Conservative Party* **manifesto** *for the 1945 election. Instead of saying 'we believe', as was usual in something written for a party, this one said 'I' – meaning Churchill.*

I had hoped the Coalition Government would continue until the end of the war with Japan. The Labour and Liberal Parties were unwilling to agree, so a general election is inevitable. I have formed a new National Government, of the best men in all parties. It is a strong government, and contains many who helped me run the country through the darkest days and on whose advice and ability I rely.

We seek the good of the whole nation. We believe the unity of the British people is greater than class or party differences. This unity enabled us to stand like a rock against Germany when she overran Europe.

Source B *Winston Churchill campaigning in London in 1945.*

The election

The Conservatives expected to win but in fact they lost. Why?

- Many people didn't trust their promises of reform. They said they would build new homes and support the poor and the unemployed. But Conservative MPs had spent years opposing such reforms in parliament.

- Many people remembered the dark days of the Depression in the 1930s and the attitudes of Conservative politicians to unemployment and poverty.

- They relied on Churchill too much, not policies.

- Labour laid out policies for change. These policies were in line with what Labour had been demanding in parliament anyway.

- Churchill, in his first election broadcast, made a huge mistake. He warned people that Labour's socialist policies were dangerous. He said you couldn't have a socialist state without a Gestapo to run it. The Gestapo were the Nazi secret police. Churchill was comparing the Labour government to the Nazis, despite the fact that the Labour leader, Clement Atlee, had been his deputy for much of the war. Their campaign never really recovered.

Exam-style question

What can you learn from Source C about what people wanted from a post-war government?

(6 marks)

Source C — *From a letter written by Dennis Healey, who became a Labour MP, to a friend in February 1945.*

I am only one of hundreds of young men, now in the forces, who long to fight an election for the Labour Party. We represent millions of soldiers, sailors and airmen who want socialism and have been fighting to save a world where socialism is possible – it is a matter of life and death for them…We have almost won the war, at the highest price ever paid for victory. If you could see the shattered misery that was once Italy: the wrecked villages; Cassino, with a bomb-created river washing green slime through rubble that once was homes; you would see that the defeat of Hitler and Mussolini is not enough to justify the destruction of twenty centuries of Europe. Only a more glorious future can make up for this wiping out of the past.

Source D — *A Labour Party poster for the 1945 election. Why does it stress the peace?*

AND NOW– WIN THE PEACE

VOTE LABOUR

Source E *From the Labour party manifesto for the 1945 election.*

They say, 'Full employment. Yes! If we can get it without interfering too much with private industry.' We say, 'Full employment in any case, and if we need to keep a firm public hand on industry in order to get jobs for all, very well. No more dole queues, in order to let the Czars of Big Business remain kings in their own castles. The price of so-called "economic freedom" for the few is too high if it is bought at the cost of idleness and misery for millions.'

Source G *Part of Clement Attlee's ironical radio reply to Source F.*

I can only suppose Mr Churchill wanted the electors to understand how great the difference is between Mr Churchill, the Great Leader in war of a united nation and Mr Churchill the Conservative party leader. He feared that those who had accepted his leadership in war might be tempted, out of gratitude, to follow him further. I thank him for having disillusioned them so thoroughly.

Source F *Part of Churchill's radio speech, 4 June 1945.*

I must tell you that a socialist policy is opposed to British ideas on freedom. There is to be one State, which all must obey. This State, once in power, will tell everyone what to do: where to work, what to work at, where they may go and what they may say, what they may think, where their wives are to queue up for the State ration, and what education their children are to receive. A socialist state could not afford opposition. No socialist system can work without a political police. They would have to fall back on some form of Gestapo.

Source H *Election results, 1945.*

Party	Number of votes	Seats in parliament
Labour	11,967,746	393
Conservative	9,101,099	197
Liberal	2,252,430	12
Others (five parties)	1,168,538	21

Activities

1. Read Source A.

   a. Write a sentence to explain how Churchill suggests a Conservative vote is a vote for the war government.

   b. Write a sentence explaining why he might think this was a good thing.

   c. Write a slogan for his election campaign, based on this part of the manifesto.

2. The cartoonist who drew Source I wanted people to realise how foolish Churchill was to suggest the Labour Party could be like the Nazi Party. List all the elements in the cartoon that make you think this.

3. Write a short paragraph for each of Sources C and I, explaining what the source tells you about why Labour came to power.

Source I *A cartoon from a British newspaper published on 7 June 1945, three days after Churchill's 'Gestapo' speech (Source F).*

The Beveridge Report

> ## Learning objectives
>
> In this chapter you will learn about:
> - the Beveridge Report and its importance
> - considering the purpose of a source.

During the war, Ernest Bevin, the minister of labour (and a member of the Labour Party) set up a committee to suggest how to improve life in Britain after the war. William Beveridge, who had worked on several committees studying social problems, was its chairman.

On 1 December 1942, the Beveridge Report, over 300 pages long, was published. Many MPs (most of them Conservative) disagreed strongly with its recommendations, but realised it had a huge amount of public support. It sold over 70,000 copies in the first few days.

The recommendations

The report said the state should support its citizens 'from the cradle to the grave' – from birth until death. It had to fight 'five giants':

- **want:** the lack of basic needs such as food
- **ignorance:** the lack of proper education for all
- **disease:** the lack of proper medical care for all
- **squalor:** poor living conditions
- **idleness:** unemployment.

As the government took control of more and more aspects of life during the war, it changed people's views on how government worked and what parts of life it was responsible for. Even Conservative MPs saw it would be harder to avoid welfare responsibilities once the war was over.

People in Britain approved of the Beveridge Report. They wanted the government to fight his giants. From the publication of the report in December 1942 up to the election of 1945, the government debated what changes to make and how to make them. During the war, it had set up free school meals and milk in 1942 as a wartime measure. After the war, it put permanent measures in place.

Source A — *Part of a radio broadcast made by William Beveridge on 2 December 1942, the day after the Beveridge Report was published. Think about who would have been listening to the broadcast.*

My report is a plan for social security. It will make sure that no one in Britain, willing to work if he can, is without enough money to meet the essential needs of himself and his family.

The scheme has three parts. Firstly, an all-in social insurance scheme of cash **benefits**. Secondly, a scheme of children's allowances, for all children. Thirdly, an all-in scheme of medical assistance at all times for everybody.

Source B — *The official notes of a Cabinet meeting on 15 February 1943. These notes were not made public until 2006.*

On 15 February, the Cabinet discussed what to say in the debate on whether to introduce legislation to give effect to the Beveridge Plan during that Parliament. It was pointed out that if they were to be ready to deal with post-war problems they needed to start planning.

The Cabinet agreed the Government should not be committed to introducing legislation for the reform of social services during the war but should not put themselves in a position where it was impossible to introduce such legislation.

Prime Minister stated: Impossible to predict the international situation after war. Make no promises; give no commitments; but make every possible preparation.

Source C · *Part of a speech by Labour MP James Griffiths during the parliamentary debate on the Beveridge Report.*

I have given the people of the town I represent a promise I must not break. I have said, 'You are asked to leave your homes, your work and your community – for the sake of the country. When the war is over I will do my best to see you are given decent jobs or, if they are not available, that you will have an income that will keep your family from want.'

Source E · *Part of a speech made by Winston Churchill at the Lord Mayor's Lunch in London on 9 November 1943.*

I regard it as a definite part of the responsibility of this National Government to have plans perfected to make sure that in the years immediately after the war, food, work and homes are found for all. The war would not be won unless there was a policy of food, work and homes after victory for the men and women who fought and won.

Source D · *A cartoon published on 17 February 1943, over two months after the Beveridge Report was published.*

Watch out!

Don't be confused by the use of the word 'idleness' in the report and elsewhere. It did not mean laziness – although it was sometimes also used in that way, especially by people who wanted to criticise the unemployed. It meant being out of work.

Exam-style question

What can you learn from Source D about reactions to the Beveridge Report? **(6 marks)**

Activities

1 Write a sentence to explain:
   - the message of Source A
   - the purpose of Source A.
2 Do the same for Sources C and D.
3 Write a sentence explaining what Source D suggests about Churchill's feeling about the Beveridge Report.
4 Does Source B support this (remember Churchill was prime minister)?

Fighting giants

> ## Learning objectives
>
> In this chapter you will learn about:
> - the attack on the five giants, especially 'want'
> - considering the purpose of a source.

In 1945 the National Government passed the Family Allowances Act. This paid 5 shillings a week for each child after the first one and the allowance was paid to mothers. Payments didn't begin until August 1945, so many people gave the newly-elected Labour government credit for it. The Labour government was elected mainly because many people felt a Conservative government would not act on Beveridge's recommendations. The Labour government went on to bring in the other measures that provided wide-ranging state support for everyone in need (see Source C).

Fighting want

Labour state support affected education, health and housing. These were all important. However, in many people's eyes the most important 'giant' was want. Labour tackled this by:

The 1946 National Insurance Act, which took NI payments from workers and employers and provided unemployment, maternity and sickness benefit. It also provided old age pensions.

The 1946 National Assistance Act, which provided National Assistance Boards to provide government help for the homeless, the disabled and the mentally ill.

For the first time there was a wide-ranging system of state support for those in need.

Source A	*This photograph, used in newspapers at the time, shows a mother and her five children at a London post office on 6 August 1946. She is collecting her first week's family allowance payment of £1 (5 shillings for each child except the eldest). Her husband, if he was an ordinary worker, would have been earning about £7 a week. Think how the extra income might have affected their lives.*

Source B *From the Daily Mail newspaper for 5 July 1948. A farm worker, among the lowest paid in 1948, earned £4 10s a week.*

On Monday morning you will wake in a new Britain, in a state that takes over its citizens six months before they are born, providing free care and services for their early years, their schooling, sickness, workless days, widowhood, retirement and death. All this with free doctoring, dentistry and medicine – all for 4s 11d of your weekly pay packet.

Activities

1 Write a paragraph explaining what Source B tells you about the Welfare State.

2 Use Source C to write an explanation of how the laws might affect:
   - an unemployed builder with four children
   - a bank manager in a small town in the south of England with two children.

3 Use the Internet to find out about the nationalisation of industries after the war.

Source C *Laws to fight the Beveridge Report giants up to 1948.*

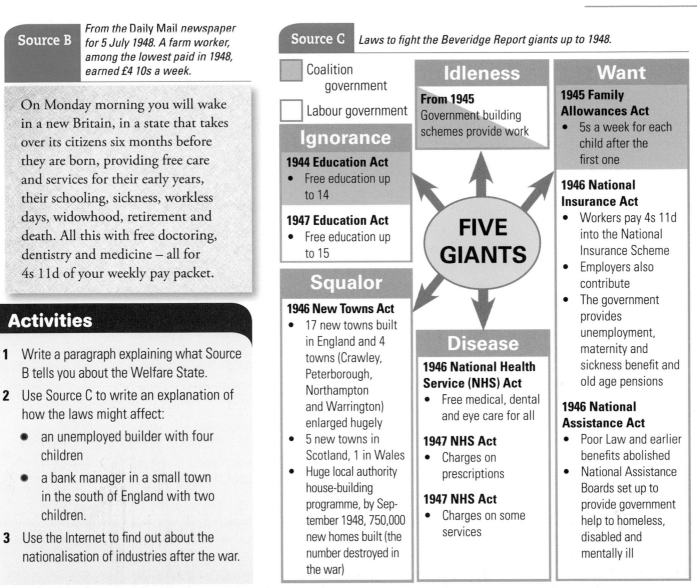

☐ Coalition government
☐ Labour government

Ignorance
1944 Education Act
- Free education up to 14

1947 Education Act
- Free education up to 15

Squalor
1946 New Towns Act
- 17 new towns built in England and 4 towns (Crawley, Peterborough, Northampton and Warrington) enlarged hugely
- 5 new towns in Scotland, 1 in Wales
- Huge local authority house-building programme, by September 1948, 750,000 new homes built (the number destroyed in the war)

Idleness
From 1945 Government building schemes provide work

FIVE GIANTS

Disease
1946 National Health Service (NHS) Act
- Free medical, dental and eye care for all

1947 NHS Act
- Charges on prescriptions

1947 NHS Act
- Charges on some services

Want
1945 Family Allowances Act
- 5s a week for each child after the first one

1946 National Insurance Act
- Workers pay 4s 11d into the National Insurance Scheme
- Employers also contribute
- The government provides unemployment, maternity and sickness benefit and old age pensions

1946 National Assistance Act
- Poor Law and earlier benefits abolished
- National Assistance Boards set up to provide government help to homeless, disabled and mentally ill

A National Health Service

> ### Learning objectives
>
> In this chapter you will learn about:
> - planning the NHS and opposition from the medical profession
> - evaluating the reliability of sources.

The Beveridge Report recommended a National Health Service that provided free medical, dental and eye care for all. It was the hardest reform for Labour to introduce. Doctors at all levels were suspicious of state control of their profession.

The BMA and the government

Many doctors belonged to the British Medical Association (BMA). It had fought government reforms, such as the 1911 introduction of free medical care (by a chosen 'panel' of doctors) for those paying NI contributions. They fought all changes to increase free health care, such as the 1941 law that raised the income of people who could claim from £250 to £420. The health service was a muddle of free 'panels', private care and hospitals and clinics run by **voluntary groups**. BMA representatives sat on government committees to discuss reform, but disagreed over the level of government control, who should get free health care and how doctors who gave it should be paid.

When Labour came to power in 1945, the new Minister of Health, Aneurin Bevan, wanted to carry out Beveridge's recommendations. He set up committees to consult with the BMA. While this was going on he pushed through the National Health Services Act (passed in November 1946), despite BMA protests. The date set for the start of free medical, dental and eye care for all was January 1948. Disputes with the BMA delayed the start date until April 1948. It was not until July 1948 that the NHS began to provide its free services.

Source A — *From a book about the development of the National Health Service written in 1988.*

The BMA had deep fears of state control. By 1943, its doctors were in confrontation with the government, not only to defend their independence, but also over past disputes. They opposed the official plan on every level. They were particularly against working for local authorities, saying this turned a profession that managed itself into a local government service.

Source B — *Written by Dr Charles Hill of the BMA, in a 1944 book on health and social welfare.*

For years, the BMA has pressed for reorganisation of the structure of the country's medical services. These have grown up, over the last hundred years, piece by piece with no co-ordination. The result is a confused muddle. A comprehensive medical service should be available to all who need it; but it is unnecessary for the state to provide it for those who can provide for themselves. The best medical service will be provided by independent professionals working with the government, rather than by doctors controlled by a bureaucracy.

Source C — *From a book about the National Health Service written in 1952.*

In January 1948, the BMA asked members: Do you approve, or disapprove, of the National Health Services Act, 1946, in its present form? The voting was 40,814 votes against and 4,735 for. On 17 March, the BMA voted not to enter the new service until it was changed. The Minister made changes to the pay and the restriction of private practice. Another vote was held. The BMA advised non-co-operation unless at least 13,000 were for it. This time the vote was 14,620 for the act with changes and 25,842 against. At a BMA meeting on 28 May it was decided to recommend doctors to take part in the service.

Source D *From the* Guardian *newspaper, 6 May 1948.*

The National Health Service is saved. A majority of doctors are still against parts of the act. But there are so many fewer against than in the February vote that the BMA has decided to advise the doctors to co-operate. It is a brave, as well as a wise, decision. It is important that people do not expect a magic change on July 5 and do not blame doctors if at first things do not work perfectly. We should be grateful that the BMA have been able to overcome their feelings of doubt and do what most people outside the profession see as the right thing.

Exam-style question

How reliable are sources C and E as evidence of doctors' opposition to the NHS? **(10 marks)**

Source E *A cartoon published in a newspaper on 15 January 1948. The person being chopped up is Bevan, the minister of health.*

OPERATION SABOTAGE

Activities

1   In pairs, discuss the message and purpose of Source E. Write a sentence to explain:
   - what bias the cartoonist has and how you know this
   - whether this bias stops the source being useful to a historian studying the NHS.
2   Write a sentence for each of the following, explaining which source you would use to show it and why:
   - why the BMA objected to the NHS Act
   - why the BMA eventually advised members to join the system.

Using the NHS

Learning objectives

In this chapter you will learn about:
● the impact of the NHS up to 1951
● evaluating a hypothesis.

At first, people could hardly believe the NHS was really going to provide health care, eye care and dental care free. They rushed to make use of it. The government had worked out their costs for the NHS on normal use of these services. This meant they badly underestimated how much it would cost. Glasses and false teeth were the most popular, but the medicine bill was also high. By 1949, the government was debating introducing charges. The National Health Service Act of 1949 set a 1-shilling prescription charge (the old, poor or disabled did not have to pay). It did not actually come into force until 1952. Bevan disagreed and resigned as Minister of Health because of it. Another Act, in 1951, put a charge of 1 shilling towards the cost of glasses or half the cost of false teeth (again, the old, poor or disabled did not have to pay). These charges were fiercely objected to, but even when they were in force, those who needed free treatment were getting it, a vast improvement on the situation before the war.

Source B	Alice Law remembers going to keep her mother company as she tried out the various services of the NHS in 1948.

Everything was just a few minutes' walk away. She went to the optician's and got new glasses on prescription from the doctor. Then she went further down the road to the chiropodist and had her feet seen to. Then she went back to the doctor, because she'd been having trouble with her ears. He said he'd fix her up with a hearing aid.

Source A	A cartoon first printed in a newspaper on 24 August 1948. The caption said: 'Absolutely free – but you'd better get cracking before the supplies run out.'

Source C	From the National Archive website article on the NHS, written in the 1990s.

Demand for health care under the new National Health Service (NHS) exceeded all predictions. The number of patients on doctors' registers rose to 30 million. The NHS budgeted £1 million for opticians, but within a year, 5.25 million prescriptions for glasses and other work had produced a bill of £32 million. In 1947, doctors wrote 7 million prescriptions a month, which rose to 19 million per month in 1951.

The poor gained access to doctors and a range of treatments previously beyond their means, and no longer needed to worry economically about illness or injury. But it was not only the poor who benefited. The middle classes also made full use of the NHS. In the first year, from a total of 240,000 hospital beds, only 2.5% were private. Over 95% of doctors joined the NHS.

Source D	From an interview with John Marks for an NHS website in 2008. Marks qualified as a doctor in 1948 and went straight to work in the NHS.

'The evening of the day the NHS started the exam results were announced. I was a doctor.'

Nine days later, John Marks registered with the General Medical Council and went straight into a job in Shoreditch at £250 a year.

'The demand when the NHS started was unbelievable. Before the health service started, there was guaranteed treatment through National Health Insurance for low-paid workers (the panel system), but even then their families were excluded. There was an enormous amount of demand for surgery for previously untreated conditions. Also for things like wigs and, in some places, free cotton wool.'

content supplied by

NHS choices ™

Source E	Government spending on the NHS each year from 1948 to 1952 (1948–9 is from July), estimate and actual.

Year	Estimated cost in £s	Actual cost in £s
1948–49	198,376,000	275,904,542
1949–50	352,324,600	449,171,732
1950–51	464,514,400	465,019,300
1951–52	469,127,700	470,551,200

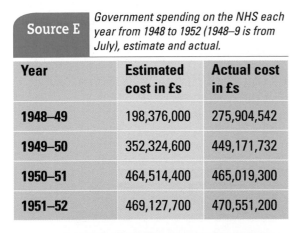

examzone

Top tip

When discussing how far sources support a statement, students will perform best if they cross-refer between sources, as well as checking each source against the statement.

examzone

Build better answers

Exam question: Use Source C and your own knowledge to explain why the NHS cost so much more than the government expected. (10 marks)

■ **A basic answer (level 1)** generalises without adequate support from source detail or own knowledge (for example, *because it was free*).

● **A good answer (level 2)** uses evidence from the source and/or own knowledge to support a reason (for example, ... *because so many more people used it than the government had budgeted for. The source actually says 'exceeded all predictions'. It is bound to cost more if more people than expected use it. Also, they probably weren't expecting such a high use of it by the middle class rather than the poor*).

▲ **An excellent answer (level 3)** uses evidence from the source and precise own knowledge to support a reason (for example, ... *because so many more people used it than they government had budgeted for. The source actually says 'exceeded all predictions'. It is bound to cost more if more people than expected use it. Also, they probably weren't expecting such a high use of it by the middle class rather than the poor – this might well be why they started to introduce charges from 1949 on (for prescriptions then towards glasses and false teeth). These charges didn't apply to the old, poor or disabled. So they were trying to get better-off users to contribute*).

Only answers that use own knowledge can reach this level.

Activities

1 Write a sentence about how far Sources C and E agree that the government could not control spending on the NHS.

2 Write a short paragraph explaining how far Sources A, B and D agree about exploitation of the NHS.

In the Unit 3 exam you will be required to answer five questions. You have 1 hour and 15 minutes to answer all five questions, so you don't need to write huge amounts. The number of marks available for each question will help you judge how much to write. The time allocation to the right gives you a little thinking time before you put pen to paper and a few minutes to read through your answers at the end. Remember that in question 5, you are also marked on spelling, punctuation and grammar, so make sure you leave enough time to check that at the end.

Question 1: 10 minutes
Question 2: 12 minutes
Question 3: 12 minutes
Question 4: 12 minutes
Question 5: 20 minutes

Here, we are going to look at Question 5. Let's use the sources in the chapter called 'Using the NHS' (on pages 72–3) to answer the sort of question you might get in an exam. There are only five sources here instead of the six in the exam, but we can still see how the levels build up.

examzone
Build better answers

Question 5

Tip: Question 5 will ask you to make a judgement about a hypothesis, using sources and your own knowledge. It will tell you to use a selection of sources and then say 'and any other sources you find helpful'. You **must** use the specified sources. However, make sure you check the other sources to see if they can help you.

In this question, it is important that you come to your own conclusion about the statement and explain how you reached this conclusion, weighing up the arguments for and against it. You can't just make something up. Consider the sources. Use your own knowledge and the captions to evaluate the sources and then use both to form a judgement about the statement.

Remember that Question 5 has 3 additional marks available for spelling, punctuation and grammar. Make sure you take extra care over the quality and accuracy of these in your answer and leave time to check it at the end.

Let's use the sources on the NHS on pages 72–73 to answer the question:

Source A suggests that people exploited the NHS when it began. How far do you agree with this interpretation? Use your own knowledge, Sources A, B and E and any other sources you find useful to explain the answer. (16 marks)

Student answer

The NHS provided free health, eye and dental treatment for everyone and many people used it.
OR
Source A shows babies with false teeth and glasses.

Comments

Both these answers can only reach level 1. The first makes a vague judgement without any detail from the sources or own knowledge to support it. The second answer produces some detail from the source, but doesn't explain how this relates to the question.

To reach level 2 the answer would have to say how far it agreed with the interpretation and then produce detail from the sources and/or own knowledge to support its view. More complete answers use evidence from the sources and own knowledge. Let's start again.

Student answer

I think Source A is strongly suggesting exploitation because babies don't need false teeth and glasses and so it is suggesting people were going to the NHS for unnecessary things because they were free. Source D suggests there was a run on wigs and cotton wool, which are hardly vital. Source B discusses one woman's use of the NHS – but this suggests she was using it rather than exploiting it. We know that many more people used it than the government was expecting, making the costs higher so they had to think about charges for some things.

Comments

This answer is much better. It uses detail from the sources and own knowledge to support a judgement on the statement. Because it uses sources and own knowledge it will be marked towards the top of level 2. A better answer would evaluate the evidence using two or more sources and/or own knowledge. Again, using sources and own knowledge will reach the top of the level. Answers will not reach level 3 unless supporting detail from sources is used.

Student answer

I think Source A is strongly suggesting exploitation because babies don't need false teeth and glasses and so it is suggesting people were going to the NHS for unnecessary things because they were free. But it is a cartoon making fun of the situation. It isn't giving you evidence (although unless there was some of this sort of thing going on it wouldn't be funny, I suppose). I think it probably was exploited, we know many more people used it than the government was expecting (like middle class people), making the costs higher so they had to think about charges for some things and introduced them (just not for the old and poor) after 1949. Source D suggests there was a run on wigs and cotton wool, which are hardly vital. Source B discusses one woman's use of the NHS – but this suggests she was using it rather than exploiting it.

Comments

This is a good level 3 answer. It makes a judgement and uses detail from several sources (including helpful detail from a source other than those listed) and own knowledge to support their view. However, they have not given a balanced answer. They haven't weighed up both sides of the argument and explained why they made the judgement they did. This would get them to level 4.

Student answer

I think there probably was some exploitation of the NHS when it began. It is only human and several sources, not just A, suggest it. Source A is strongly suggesting exploitation because babies don't need false teeth and glasses and so it is suggesting people were going to the NHS for unnecessary things because they were free. But it is a cartoon making fun of the situation. It isn't giving you evidence (although unless there was some of this sort of thing going on it wouldn't be funny). I suppose it depends on how you define exploitation, too. Source D suggests there was a run on wigs and cotton wool, which some might say are hardly vital, but people could argue they were paying NI contributions so were entitled to it for free. Source B discusses one woman's use of the NHS – but this suggests she was using it as much as she could rather than exploiting it (though a daughter talking about her mother might make it seem like that). We know many more people used it than the government was expecting (like middle class people), making the costs higher so they had to think about charges for some things and introduce them (just not for the old and poor) after 1949. But was this exploitation? They said the NHS was providing free health care for all, not just for the poor and old etc. So it's not exploitation to use something your NI contributions pay for, even if you could afford to pay to not use the NHS, besides most doctors were part of the scheme anyway.

Comments

This answer explores arguments for and against the interpretation, supporting it with detail from own knowledge and several sources. It clearly states its judgement and explains why.

Welcome to exam

Revising for your exams can be a daunting prospect. Use this section of the book to get ideas, tips and practice to help you prepare as best as you can.

Zone In!

Have you ever become so absorbed in a task that it suddenly feels entirely natural? This is a feeling familiar to many athletes and performers: it's a feeling of being 'in the zone' that helps you focus and achieve your best.

Here are our top tips for getting in the zone with your revision.

● **Understand the exam process** and what revision you need to do. This will give you confidence but also help you to put things into proportion. Use the Planning Zone to create a revision plan.

● **Build your confidence** by using your revision time, not just to revise the information you need to know, but also to practise the skills you need for the examination. Try answering questions in timed conditions so that you're more prepared for writing answers in the exam.

● **Deal with distractions** by making a list of everything that might interfere with your revision and how you can deal with each issue. For example, revise in a room without a television, but plan breaks in your revision so that you can watch your favourite programmes.

● **Share your plan with friends and family** so that they know not to distract you when you want to revise. This will mean you can have more quality time with them when you aren't revising.

● **Keep healthy** by making sure you eat well and exercise, and by getting enough sleep. If your body is not in the right state, your mind won't be either – and staying up late to cram the night before the exam is likely to leave you too tired to do your best.

Planning Zone

The key to success in exams and revision often lies in the right planning, so that you don't leave anything until the last minute. Use these ideas to create your personal revision plan.

First, fill in the dates of your examinations. Check with your teacher when these are if you're not sure. Add in any regular commitments you have. This will help you get a realistic idea of how much time you have to revise.

Know your strengths and weaknesses and assign more time to topics you find difficult – don't be tempted to leave them until the last minute.

Create a revision 'checklist' using the Know Zone lists and use them to check your knowledge and skills.

Now fill in the timetable with sensible revision slots. Chunk your revision into smaller sections to make it more manageable and less daunting. Make sure you give yourself regular breaks and plan in different activities to provide some variety.

Keep to the timetable! Put your plan up somewhere visible so you can refer back to it and check that you are on track.

Know Zone

In this zone, you'll find checklists to help you review what you've learned and which areas you still need to work on.

Test your knowledge

Use these checklists to test your knowledge of the main areas for each topic. If you find gaps or weaknesses in your knowledge, refer back to the relevant pages of the book.

Key Topic 1

You should know about...

❑ Levels and distribution of unemployment in Britain in the 1930s **see pages 10–11**

❑ How the government tried to deal with the problems of unemployment **see pages 12–13**

❑ Experiences of the unemployed **see pages 14–15**

❑ The reasons for the Jarrow Crusade, how it was organised and opposition to it **see pages 16–17**

❑ The marchers; their effect on public opinion **see pages 18–19**

❑ The effects of the Jarrow Crusade **see pages 20–21**

Key Topic 2

You should know about...

❑ The events at the start of the Second World War **see page 25**

❑ The German invasion of the Netherlands, Belgium and France and the retreat of the BEF **see pages 26–27**

❑ The importance of Dunkirk and the reasons for British survival **see pages 28–29**

❑ The reasons for the Battle of Britain and its importance **see pages 30–31**

❑ Preparation for D-Day and events **see pages 32–33**

❑ Reasons for the success of D-Day **see pages 34–35**

❑ The defeat of Germany **see pages 36–37**

Key Topic 3

You should know about...

- ❏ Government preparation for attacks on Britain **see pages 41–43**
- ❏ The evacuation of the cities **see pages 44–45**
- ❏ The Blitz and its effects generally **see pages 46–47**
- ❏ The Blitz on Coventry **see pages 48–49**
- ❏ How German bombing changed and developed after the Blitz **see pages 50–51**
- ❏ The use of censorship and propaganda **see pages 52–53**
- ❏ The impact of the war on the food supply and how the government dealt with it **see pages 54–55**
- ❏ The war work women did **see pages 56–57**
- ❏ How women's war work affected post-war employment **see pages 58–59**

Key Topic 4

You should know about...

- ❏ Why Labour won the 1945 election **see pages 63–65**
- ❏ The Beveridge Report and its importance **see pages 66–67**
- ❏ The attack on the five giants, especially 'want' **see pages 68–69**
- ❏ Planning the NHS and opposition from the medical profession **see pages 70–71**
- ❏ The impact of the NHS up to 1951 **see pages 72–73**

Working with sources

Remember, however, that this unit is not just about recalling historical information: you need to be able to interpret and make judgements about historical sources.

As you've studied each topic, you'll have built up a range of skills for working with sources. The table below lists the main areas you should now feel confident in and shows where each is covered in the book. Refer back to those pages during your revision to check and practise your source skills.

	Key Topic 1	Key Topic 2	Key Topic 3	Key Topic 4
Making inferences from sources	pages 11 and 20		page 47	
Considering the purpose of a source	page 17	page 37	page 49	Pages 68–69
Explaining causation using a source and own knowledge	page 19	page 31	pages 53 and 57	
Evaluating the reliability of sources	page 13	pages 29 and 35		
Evaluating a hypothesis		page 39		Pages 72–73

Exam Zone Unit 3B Practice exam paper

Here is a practice paper for the Unit 3B exam. The sources that you need to read to answer these questions are provided on pages 80–81. In Unit 3 you have to answer all five questions.

Each question will tell you which source or sources you need to read and refer to. The number of marks available for each question is given on the right. Remember that the Unit 3 exam lasts 1 hour 15 minutes. Plan your time accordingly!

Question 1
Study Source A.
What can you learn about the reasons for the Blitz from Source A? (6)

Question 2
Study Source B and use your own knowledge.
What was the purpose of this representation?
Use details from the poster and your own knowledge to explain your answer. (8)

Question 3
Study Source B and use your own knowledge.
Use Source B and your own knowledge to explain why the government wanted to evacuate children from major cities. (10)

Question 4
Study Sources C and D and use your own knowledge.
How reliable are Sources C and D as evidence of morale in London during the Blitz?
Explain your answer, using Sources D and E and your own knowledge. (10)

Question 5
Source C suggests that civilian morale held up well during the Blitz. How far do you agree with this interpretation? Use your own knowledge, Sources C, D and E and any other sources you find useful to explain your answer.
Spelling, punctuation and grammar will be assessed in this question. (16)

Background information

The Blitz is the name given to the bombing of British cities by the *Luftwaffe* from 7 September 1940 to May 1941. It was different from previous bombing raids because it deliberately targeted civilians, not military or industrial targets. The government took many precautions against bombing from the start of the war, including evacuating children. The first, most-often and most-heavily bombed city was London – it was bombed for 75 out of the first 76 nights of bombing (one night it was too foggy to fly). There were bombing raids on many other British cities, for example Coventry and Liverpool. The government worked hard to 'keep up morale' – keep people determined to carry on fighting – despite the bombing.

Source A   From a school textbook published in 1988.

To start with, the *Luftwaffe* [German air force] concentrated on destroying airfields as part of its invasion plan. In September, this policy was switched to one of bombing London. Having failed to beat the RAF [the British air force], *Luftwaffe* planes could only attack at night, when it was harder for the RAF to shoot them down. Bombing cities was intended to break the morale of the British and make them want peace at any price.

Source B   A poster issued by the government in 1940.

LEAVE THIS TO US SONNY — <u>YOU</u> OUGHT TO BE OUT OF LONDON

MINISTRY OF HEALTH EVACUATION SCHEME

Exam Zone

Source C   From the diary of Maggie Joy Blunt, who lived about 20 miles from London, 9 September 1940.

Raids over London are constant and seem to get worse and worse. Damage and death over the docks and East End have been terrible. But Hitler won't win. We will not be subdued. We will have a better world. Damnation to those who machine–gun our women and children, and they do. Only last week a hundred or more factory girls were killed in this way in their lunch hour.

Source D   From the diary of Christopher Tomalin, a 28-year-old who lived with his parents in London, 15 September 1940.

Our only shelter from the bombing is the pantry under the stairs: one wall is an outside wall; the other is thin board. I am scared by the indiscriminate night bombing of London and the rest of England. It is obvious the RAF and the anti-aircraft people can't do much about it. We can beat them in daylight, but not when it's dark. How can I, or anyone, sleep under these conditions?

Source E   A postman delivering mail in London, May 1941.

Source F   From a speech by the British prime minister, Winston Churchill, on 14 July 1941, after the Blitz.

I do not hesitate to say that the enormous change in the opinion of the people of the United States towards making a greater, more effective contribution to British resistance has been largely influenced by the behaviour of Londoners (and the men and women of other cities) in standing up to enemy bombing.

Don't Panic Zone

As the day of the exam gets closer, many students tend to go into panic mode, either working long hours without really giving their brain a chance to absorb information, or giving up and staring blankly at the wall.

Look over your revision notes and go through the checklists in Know Zone to remind yourself of the main areas you need to know about. Don't try to cram in too much new information at the last minute and don't stay up late revising – you'll do better if you get a good night's sleep.

Exam Zone

What to expect in the exam paper

You will have 1 hour and 15 minutes in the examination. There will be five questions and you should answer all of these. There will be between six and eight sources in a separate source booklet; some of these will be written and some will be illustrations.

Question 1 is an inference question worth 6 marks. It will ask what a source is suggesting, usually phrased as 'What can you learn from Source X?' You should spend about 10 minutes on this question. For an example, see page 22.

Question 2 is a source analysis question worth 8 marks. It will ask you about the purpose of the source, for example 'Why was the source produced?' or 'Why was this photograph used?' You should spend about 12 minutes on this question. You must refer to the source and your own knowledge in this question. For an example, see page 23.

Question 3 is worth 10 marks and involves explaining causation using a source and your own knowledge. The question will usually be in the form 'Use Source A and your own knowledge to explain why …' You cannot reach the highest level without using detail from your own knowledge. You should spend about 12 minutes on this question. For an example, see pages 42–43.

Question 4 is worth 10 marks and asks you to evaluate the reliability of two sources, using the sources and your own knowledge. It is important to evaluate both sources and use supporting detail from your own knowledge. It is usually phrased as 'How reliable are Sources A and B as evidence of …?' You should spend about 12 minutes on this question. For an example, see pages 58–59.

Question 5 is a judgement question worth 16 marks. It will start with giving you an interpretation from a source used in the paper and then ask 'How far do you agree with this interpretation?' You will need to use your own knowledge, all the sources specified and any other sources you find useful to explain your answer. Remember there are up to 3 additional marks for spelling, punctuation and grammar for your answer to this question. You should spend about 20 minutes on this question. For an example, see pages 72–73.

Meet the exam paper

This diagram shows the front cover of the exam paper. These instructions, information and advice will always appear on the front of the paper. It is worth reading it carefully now. Check you understand it and ask your teacher about anything you are not sure of.

Print your surname here, and your other names afterwards. This is an additional safeguard to ensure that the exam board awards the marks to the right candidate.

Here you fill in the school's exam number.

The Unit 3 exam lasts 1 hour 15 minutes. Plan your time accordingly.

Make sure that you answer all questions.

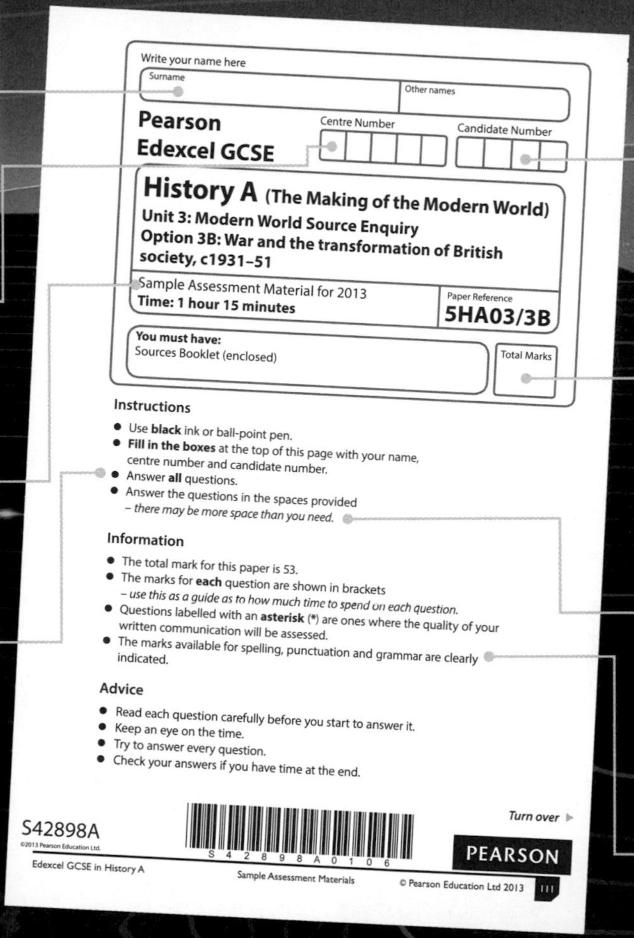

Here you fill in your personal exam number. Take care to write it accurately.

In this box, the examiner will write the total marks you have achieved in the exam paper.

Don't feel that you have to fill the answer space provided. Everybody's handwriting varies, so a long answer from you may take up as much space a short answer from someone else.

Remember that in Question 5 the quality of your written communication will be assessed. Take time to check your spelling, punctuation and grammar and to make sure that you have expressed yourself clearly.

Write your name here

Surname

Other names

**Pearson
Edexcel GCSE**

Centre Number

Candidate Number

History A (The Making of the Modern World)

**Unit 3: Modern World Source Enquiry
Option 3B: War and the transformation of British society, c1931–51**

Sample Assessment Material for 2013
Time: 1 hour 15 minutes

Paper Reference

5HA03/3B

You must have:
Sources Booklet (enclosed)

Total Marks

Instructions

- Use **black** ink or ball-point pen.
- **Fill in the boxes** at the top of this page with your name, centre number and candidate number.
- Answer **all** questions.
- Answer the questions in the spaces provided
  – there may be more space than you need.

Information

- The total mark for this paper is 53.
- The marks for **each** question are shown in brackets
  – use this as a guide as to how much time to spend on each question.
- Questions labelled with an **asterisk** (*) are ones where the quality of your written communication will be assessed.
- The marks available for spelling, punctuation and grammar are clearly indicated.

Advice

- Read each question carefully before you start to answer it.
- Keep an eye on the time.
- Try to answer every question.
- Check your answers if you have time at the end.

S42898A
©2013 Pearson Education Ltd.

Edexcel GCSE in History A

Sample Assessment Materials

Turn over ▶

PEARSON

© Pearson Education Ltd 2013

Answer ALL questions.

Look carefully at Sources A to F in the Sources Booklet and then answer Questions 1 to 5 which follow.

1   Study Source A.

What can you learn from Source A about the German bombing raid on Coventry, November 1940?

(6)

The live question paper will contain one further page of lines.

(Total for Question 1 = 6 marks)

In Unit 3 you need to answer all five questions on the paper.

Each question will tell you which source or sources you need to read in the sources booklet.

The number of marks available for each question is given on the right.

Historical Enquiry: The impact of the Blitz

Source A: From a broadcast on Berlin Radio, 16 November 1940, about the German air raid on Coventry.

More than 500 planes took part in the greatest attack in the history of aerial warfare. About 500 tonnes of high-explosive bombs and 30,000 incendiary bombs were dropped. In a short time all large and small factories were set on fire and the *Luftwaffe* heavy calibre bombs caused extensive damage to other targets of military importance.

Source B: From an article published in a British newspaper, the *Daily Herald*, 16 November 1940. This article is a representation of the bombing of Coventry.

Coventry

The bombing of Coventry was as foul a deed as Hitler ever ordered. His airmen were instructed: 'Don't worry if you cannot reach your industrial targets. Bomb and burn the city. Never mind if you hit factories. Hit houses. Have no scruples about military objectives. Kill men, kill women, kill children. Destroy! Destroy! Destroy!'

Heil Hitler! Heil bloodshed! Heil pain!

Read the detail about the origin and date of each source carefully before studying the source.

Zone Out

This section provides answers to the most common questions students have about what happens after they complete their exams. For more information, visit www.examzone.co.uk.

When will my results be published?

Results for GCSE examinations are issued on the third Thursday in August.

Can I get my results online?

Visit www.resultsplusdirect.co.uk, where you will find detailed student results information including the 'Edexcel Gradeometer', which demonstrates how close you were to the nearest grade boundary.

I haven't done as well as I expected. What can I do now?

First of all, talk to your teacher. After all the teaching that you have had, and the tests and internal examinations you have done, he/she is the person who best knows what grade you are capable of achieving. Take your results slip to your subject teacher, and go through the information on it in detail. If you both think that there is something wrong with the result, the school or college can apply to see your completed examination paper and then, if necessary, ask for a re-mark immediately.

Can I have a re-mark of my examination paper?

Yes, this is possible, but remember only your school or college can apply for a re-mark, not you or your parents/carers. First of all you should consider carefully whether or not to ask your school or college to make a request for a re-mark. It is worth knowing that very few re-marks result in a change to a grade, simply because a re-mark request has shown that the original marking was accurate. Check the closing date for re-marking requests with your Examinations Officer.

Bear in mind that there is no guarantee that your grades will go up if your papers are re-marked. The original mark can be confirmed or lowered, as well as raised, as a result of a re-mark.

Glossary

Term	Definition
air raid shelter	Somewhere built, usually underground, where people can go to be safer from bombing.
Allies	Allies are people or countries who work together. In the Second World War, the 'Allies' was the name given to the countries that fought together against Germany and its allies.
artillery	Large guns or cannon, that fire over long distances.
bailed out	Said by pilots about jumping out of a plane, usually with a parachute, while the plane is still in the air.
barrage balloons	Large balloons, fixed in place with ropes or cables, that were flown above important places to stop the enemy flying low enough to bomb them accurately.
blackout	Not showing lights anywhere at night – covering doors and windows, turning out street lights, etc.
Blitz	The name given to the bombing of British cities by the German air force from 7 September 1940 to May 1941.
Cabinet (the)	The prime minister of Britain and senior government ministers meeting regularly to make decisions.
censorship	Stopping people from passing on certain information – in newspapers, radio broadcasts, private letters and even conversations.
conscription	Making people join the armed forces or do war work.
Depression (the)	The period after the Wall Street Crash in the USA when world economies were all in trouble and there was a lot of hardship and unemployment.
eligible	Qualified to get or apply for something.
Employment Exchange	A place where unemployed people went to register as available for work and to see if there were any jobs.
evacuate	To evacuate a place is to clear people out of it.
evacuee	Someone who is evacuated – sent away from a dangerous place.
hunger marches	The name given to various marches in the 1930s by unemployed people hoping to be given work or other help.
imported	To buy something from another country.
manifesto	A list of the political beliefs of a person or group of people.

means test	The inspection that people had to go through to show they were poor enough to qualify for 'the dole' – state assistance for the very poor.
minister	The person in the government in charge of a ministry, for example the Ministry of Education.
ministry	The place where people run all the government work to do with one particular area of life, for example education.
propaganda	Giving people information in order to make them think or behave in a particular way.
public baths	Places with washing facilities (sinks and baths) for people with none of their own to use.
public meeting	A meeting in a public place that anyone can go to.
radar	Short for **RA**dio **D**etection **A**nd **R**anging, a way of detecting objects a long way away in the dark or fog by bouncing radio waves off them and picking up a picture of their shape.
rationing	Restricting how much of something people can have.
refugee	A person who has been driven out of their home/country, usually by war or persecution.
relief	In this sense, it means help given to people who are homeless or desperately poor.
sandbag	A bag made from cheap sack-type fabric, about the size of a pillowcase, filled with earth or sand. Sandbags are stacked up against buildings to lessen the damage done in flooding or by an explosion.
trade union	An organisation of workers set up to help protect their rights.
Treaty of Versailles	The treaty between Germany and the Allies at the end of the First World War that limited Germany's armed services and took away much of the land Germany took in that war.
voluntary group	A group of people who work at something or provide some kind of service for free.
workhouse	A place where homeless people could live, but where families were split up, the work was hard and people were fed very little food of the cheapest sort.

Published by Pearson Education Limited, Edinburgh Gate, Harlow, Essex, CM20 2JE.

www.pearsonschoolsandfecolleges.co.uk

Copies of official specifications for all Edexcel qualifications may be found on the Edexcel website: www.edexcel.com

Text © Pearson Education Limited 2013
Typeset by HL Studios, Witney, Oxford
Illustrated by Peter Bull Studio
Cover photo/illustration © **Front:** Mirrorpix

The rights of Jane Shuter and Nigel Kelly to be identified as authors of this work have been asserted by them in accordance with the Copyright, Designs and Patents Act 1988.

First published 2013

16 15 14
10 9 8 7 6 5 4 3

British Library Cataloguing in Publication Data
A catalogue record for this book is available from the British Library

ISBN 978 1 446 90676 7

Acknowledgements
The author and publisher would like to thank the following individuals and organisations for permission to reproduce photographs:

(Key: b-bottom; c-centre; l-left; r-right; t-top)
akg-images Ltd: 26, 47; **Bridgeman Art Library Ltd:** Colin Moss 6, 19, E. H. Henington 13, Royal Naval Museum, Portsmouth, Hampshire, UK 53r, Bert Thomas 41; **Corbis:** Bettmann 9, 24, 44, 48, Hulton-Deutsch Collection 7, 8, 11, 17, 18, 20, 52, 57, 62, 68, 81, David Pollack 25, Underwood & Underwood 63; **Getty Images:** Central Press 49, Fox Photos / Harry Todd 40, 56, Picture Post / Kurt Hutton 15, Popperfoto 51, Popperfoto / Rolls Press 35, Topical Press Agency / Edward G. Malindine 58, Topical Press Agency / Warburton 59; **Imperial War Museum:** 43, Cundall, Charles Ernest RA 28; **nisyndication.com:** 21; **Solo Syndication / Associated Newspapers Ltd:** 31, 65, 67, 71, 72, Associated Newspapers Ltd 37, 50; **The Art Archive:** Bodleian Library Oxford 64, Eileen Tweedy 53l, 55; **TopFoto:** HIP / The Lordprice Collection 80

We are grateful to the following for permission to reproduce copyright material:

Tables
Source A, page 10 from *British Unemployment 1919-1939 (1990) Table 2, p5 (adapted)* 1990 Cambridge University Press (W R Garside); Table on page 15 from *The Twentieth Century, Macmillan Education (Hamer, J. 1988) pp. 106-7*; Source A, page 16 from *Modern World History, Heinemann (Hewitt, T. and Shuter, J. 2001) p. 270*, Pearson Oxford

Text
Source A, page 12 from *Unemployment HC Deb 04 November 1932 vol 269 cc2127-210* http://hansard.millbanksystems.com/commons/1932/nov/04/unemployment (George Lansbury) 4 November 1932, Open Parliament Licence: Contains Parliamentary information licensed under the Open Parliament Licence v1.0; Source A, page 14 from *Road to Wigan Pier* ISBN-13: 978-0141185293 *Page 73* Penguin Classics (George Orwell) 26 April 2001, The Road To Wigan Pier by George Orwell (Copyright © George Orwell, 1937) reprinted by permission of Bill Hamilton as the Literary Executor of the Estate of the Late Sonia Brownell Orwell and From THE ROAD TO WIGAN PIER by George Orwell © 1958 and renewed by the Estate of Sonia B. Orwell, reprinted by permission of Houghton Publishing Company. All rights reserved; Source B, page 14 from Extracts from the Pilgrim Trust Unemployment Enquiry, 1936-1938 (AST 7/255) http://www.nationalarchives.gov.uk/education/topics/going-short.htm, The National Archives: Crown Copyright / Open Government Licence; Source C, page 21 from Unemployment (Jarrow) HC Deb 05 November 1986 vol 103 cc1058-66 http://hansard.millbanksystems.com/commons/1986/nov/05/unemployment-jarrow, Don Dixon MP 05 November 1986, Open Parliament Licence: Contains Parliamentary information licensed under the Open Government Licence v1.0; Source A, page 26 from a story written by Agnis van Loon, reprinted by permission of Trevor Griffin; Source C, page 29 from Winston Churchill, speech 4th June 1940, reproduced with permission of Curtis Brown, London on behalf of the Estate of Sir Winston ; Churchill ; Source D, page 29 after *The Evacuation from Dunkirk: 'Operation Dynamo', 26 May-June 1940* ISBN-13: 978-0714681504 Naval Staff Histories Routledge; First edition July 1, 2000, Crown Copyright, Open Government Licence; Source A, page 30 from *An article about Frank Walker-Smith, Derby Evening Telegraph, 2001 (Slater, B.)*; Source B, page 31 from http://www.bbm.org.uk/Wlasnowolski.htm, Battle of Britain Archive 2007, Courtesy of www.bbm.org.uk; Source D, page 35 from Winston Churchill, Speech to the House of Commons 6th June 1944, reproduced with permission of Curtis Brown, London on behalf of the Estate of Sir WinstonChurchill ; Source A, page 42 from *Pat Ashford from Mass-Observation diary, August and September 1939*, Curtis Brown (for Mass-Observation Archive); Source B, page 43 from *Eileen Potter from Mass-Observation diary, 25 June*

1940, Curtis Brown (for Mass-Observation Archive); Source C, page 43 from *Edward Ward from Mass-Observation diary, 8 August 1940*, Curtis Brown (for Mass-Observation Archive); Source C, page 45 from *Eileen Potter from Mass-Observation diary, September 1939*, Curtis Brown (for Mass-Observation Archive); Source D, page 45 from *Evacuees in World War Two - the True Story by David Prest*; Source E, page 45 from *Tilly Rice from Mass-Observation diary, 5 December 1939 and 6 February 1940*, Curtis Brown (for Mass-Observation Archive); Source A, page 46 from *New Yorker magazine* (Mollie Panter-Downes), 14 September 1940; Source B, page 47, page 81 from *Christopher Tomalin from Mass-Observation diary, 15 September 1940*, Curtis Brown (for Mass-Observation Archive); Source C, page 47 from *Pam Ashford from Mass-Observation diary, 15 September 1940*, Curtis Brown (for Mass-Observation Archive); Source B, page 48 from *The Account of Ted Simmonds* (Pam Crane) with kind permission from Rev. Pam Crane; Source C, page 49 from Coventry's ordeal/ Ruthless bombing | Dusk-to-dawn attacks, *The Guardian*, The Guardian http://century.guardian.co.uk/1940-1949/Story/0,127361,00.html; Source A, page 50 from *Joyce's War, 1939-45 ISBN-13: 978-1853815133* Virago Press (Joyce Storey) 3 Sep 1992; Source B, page 50 from *Maggie Joy Blunt from Mass-Observation diary, 25 June 1944*, Curtis Brown (for Mass-Observation Archive); Source C, page 51 from *Edward Stebbing from Mass-Observation diary, June 1944*, Curtis Brown (for Mass-Observation Archive); Source A, page 52 from Churchill's top secret call girl, *Daily Mail*, 10 October 2008 (Hennessy, V.); Source C, page 53 from Make Do and Mend, prepared for the Board of Trade by the Ministry of Information Her Majesty's Stationery Office (HMSO) Crown Copyright material is reproduced with the permission of the Controller of HMSO and the Queen's Printer for Scotland, contains public sector information licensed under the Open Government Licence (OGL) v1.0.http://www.nationalarchives.gov.uk/doc/open-government-licence; Source C, page 55 from *Mrs. Milburn's Diaries: An Englishwoman's Day to Day Reflections, 1939-45 ISBN-13: 978-0349106236* Abacus (Clara Emily Milburn); Source B, page 57 from *Instructions for American Servicemen in Britain, 1942: Reproduced from the Original Typescript, War Department, Washington, DC (Instructions for Servicemen) ISBN-13: 978-1851240852* The Bodleian Library 1 Sep 2004; Source C, page 58 from *Out of the Cage: Women's Experiences in Two World Wars P260 ISBN-13: 978-0415622677* Routledge (Gail Braybon and Penny Summerfield) 10 Oct 2012; Source A, page 63 from Conservative Party manifesto 1945, With kind permission of the Conservative Party Archive; Source F, page 65 from Winston Churchill Radio speech, 04/06/1945, reproduced with permission of Curtis Brown, London on behalf of the Estate of Sir Winston ; Churchill ; Source A, page 66 from Beveridge radio report, William Beveridge, Liberal Democrats, 2 December 1942; Source B, page 66 from The official notes of a Cabinet meeting on 15 February 1943, http://www.nationalarchives.gov.uk/releases/2006/january/january1/default.htm Her Majesty's Stationery Office (HMSO) Parliamentary material is reproduced with the permission of the Controller of HMSO on behalf of Parliament, contains public sector information licensed under the Open Government Licence (OGL) v1.0.http://www.nationalarchives.gov.uk/doc/open-government-licence; Source C, page 67 from James Griffiths MP, speech: Social Insurance and Allied Services. HC Deb 18 February 1943 vol 386 cc1964-2054, http://hansard.millbanksystems.com/commons/1943/feb/18/social-insurance-and-allied-services Her Majesty's Stationery Office (HMSO) Parliamentary material is reproduced with the permission of the Controller of HMSO on behalf of Parliament, contains public sector information licensed under the Open Government Licence (OGL) v1.0.http://www.nationalarchives.gov.uk/doc/open-government-licence; Source E, on page 67 from Winston Churchill at the Lord Mayor's lunch in London, 09/11/1943, reproduced with permission of Curtis Brown, London on behalf of the Estate of Sir Winston Churchill; Source B on page 69 from On Monday morning you will wake in a new Britain, Daily Mail, 5th July 1948; Source A, page 70 from The Health Services Since the War, Vol 1, Charles Webster, HMSO, 1988, ISBN 978-0116309426, p.48, Contains public sector information licensed under the Open Government Licence (OGL) v1.0.http://www.nationalarchives.gov.uk/doc/open-government-licence.; Source B, page 70 from Origins of the NHS http://www.nationalarchives.gov.uk/cabinetpapers/alevelstudies/origins-nhs.htm Crown copyright protected material; Source C, page 70 from *The National Health Service in Great Britain: An historical and descriptive study ASIN: B0000CIC30*, OUP (James Stirling Ross 1952) pp125, 126, by permission of Oxford University Press; Source D, page 71 from More Doctors Back NHS, *The Guardian*, http://century.guardian.co.uk/1940-1949/Story/0,105133,00.html Thursday 6 May 1948, Guardian News and Media Ltd with permission; Source B, page 72 from *Yesterday's Britain: The Illustrated Story of How We Lived, Worked and Played in this Century ISBN-13: 978-0276423918*, Reader's Digest (1998) p.189, permission granted by 'The Reader's Digest Association Inc'; Source D, page 73 from NHS Choices, Dr John Marks at http://www.nhs.uk/Livewell/NHS60/Pages/JohnHenryMarks.aspx, reproduced by kind permission of the Department ; of Health, © 2013; Source C, page 81 from *Maggie Joy Blunt from Mass-Observation diary, 9 September 1940*, Curtis Brown (for Mass-Observation Archive); Source D, page 81 from *Christopher Tomalin from Mass-Observation diary, 15 September 1940*, Curtis Brown (for Mass-Observation Archive); Source F, page 81 from Winston Churchill 14/07/1941, Reproduced with permission of Curtis Brown, London on behalf of the Estate of Sir Winston; Churchill

A note from the publisher
In order to ensure that this student book offers high-quality support for the associated Edexcel qualification, it has been through a review process by the awarding organisation to confirm that it fully covers the teaching and learning content of the specification or part of a specification at which it is aimed, and demonstrates an appropriate balance between the development of subject skills, knowledge and understanding, in addition to preparation for assessment.

While the publishers have made every attempt to ensure that advice on the qualification and its assessment is accurate, the official specification and associated assessment guidance materials are the only authoritative source of information and should always be referred to for definitive guidance.

Edexcel examiners have not contributed to any updated sections in this resource relevant to examination papers for which they have responsibility.

No material from an endorsed student book will be used verbatim in any assessment set by Edexcel.

Endorsement of a student book does not mean that the student book is required to achieve this Edexcel qualification, nor does it mean that it is the only suitable material available to support the qualification, and any resource lists produced by the awarding organisation shall include this and other appropriate resources.